BIRNBAUM'S

Walt Disney World®

2025-2026 THE OFFICIAL GUIDE FOR KIDS

Wendy Lefkon EDITORIAL DIRECTOR

Jessica Ward EDITOR

Disney Editions Design Team DESIGNER

Alexandra Mayes Birnbaum CONSULTING EDITOR

Disney

EDITIONS

LOS ANGELES • NEW YORK

For Steve, who made all of this possible.

ISBN: 978-1-368-10499-9
FAC-023274-25205
First Edition, October 2025
10 9 8 7 6 5 4 3 2 1

Printed in the United States of America

An enormous debt of gratitude is owed to Warren Meislin, Jerry Gonzalez, Jennifer Eastwood, Julie Rose, Monica Vasquez,
Jill Safro, Amy Henning, Reid Henning, Jilly Bean Kunkel, Dan Kunkel, Matt Stroshane, and the Walt Disney World team for
making this book possible.

Other 2025–2026 Birnbaum's Official Disney Guides:
Walt Disney World and *Disneyland*

Contents

© Disney

You're Going to
DISNEY WORLD!

When you first heard the news, you could not believe your ears. Could it be true? Were you really going on a vacation to Walt Disney World? Well, believe it or not, it's true! Before you know it, you will be in the sunny state of Florida. It's the home of Walt Disney World and the most famous mouse on planet Earth. (Big hint: His name starts with M.)

If you have ever been there, you already know that it is a mighty big place with lots of stuff to do. In fact, there is so much going on that it can get a little confusing. That's where this book comes in handy. It describes everything in the World, from the Magic Kingdom theme park to yummy meals with Disney pals. And it's filled with advice from kids like you.

There is no right or wrong way to read this book. You can start on the first page and read straight through to the end. Or you can skip around, read your favorite parts first, and come back to the rest later.

No matter what you do, one thing is for sure: When you are done, you will be a true-blue Walt Disney World expert. Soon folks may start asking YOU for advice on how to have the most awesome vacation at Walt Disney World!

Pack a Pen and Take Me Along with You

Don't leave this book behind when you head for the parks. It is full of tips and information that you will want to remember. There are pages for photos and autographs, too — don't forget to bring a pen and your camera. Here are some ways to use this book while visiting the wonderful world of Disney:

Track Your Trip

Each time you check out a Walt Disney World attraction, check it off in this book. Then you'll know what's left for your next visit!

We're Warning You!

Disney rides are full of surprises. That's part of what makes them so much fun. But not everyone enjoys surprises. If things like loud noises or wild turns scare you, look at the book's attraction reaction warnings before you go on each ride. That way, the only surprises you come across will be good ones!

WILD   LOUD   DARK

SCARY   WET

Line Time

Nearly every Disney attraction has a standby line. That's where you wait until it's your turn to ride. Those lines are available to everyone — and can get a bit long sometimes. That's when it's fun to pass the time playing games such as I Spy or the Disney alphabet game — A is for Aladdin, B is for Bambi, and so on. (Read more about "waiting games" on page 131.) Another way to enter an attraction is to use the Lightning Lane — a service that offers a shorter line for an extra cost. To learn about Lightning Lanes, ask a parent or guardian to visit *disneyworld.com*.

Search for Hidden Mickeys

Disney Imagineers have hidden images of Mickey Mouse all over Walt Disney World. (Many look like the three connected circles that form Mickey's head.) You might see them in shadows, lights, drawings, or even in the clouds at some attractions. Look in this book for each **HIDDEN MICKEY ALERT!** to find a clue. Keep track of the number of Hidden Mickeys that you discover. When your Walt Disney World trip is over, write that number on page 149 of this book's Magical Memories section.

The last pages of this book are for autographs!

Meet the Readers

What do the kids who helped with this book have in common? They love Walt Disney World! How do we know? They told us so! Every kid who wrote to us last year received a survey form. The surveys came back filled with opinions about Walt Disney World. The forms also helped us find out about readers' interests and hobbies.

What did we learn? For starters, a lot of you enjoy reading, writing, playing sports, making music, and using computers. You also like to draw, sing, and dance. Your top Disney hotels are the Polynesian Village, Beach Club, Art of Animation, and Animal Kingdom Lodge. Not all of you are crazy about dark or scary rides. But wild rides like Expedition Everest, Space Mountain, and Big Thunder Mountain are at the top of your list. You think Blizzard Beach is the perfect place to splash around. And when your tummy rumbles, you reach for a frozen pineapple treat called Dole Whip, a Mickey Mouse ice cream bar, a Mickey ice cream sandwich, or a Mickey-shaped pretzel. Yum!

To everyone who filled out a survey form, THANK YOU! This book could not have been written without you. And feel free to write again. We love to hear from our readers!

—The Editors

Mickey Is Number One!

It's probably not a big surprise to hear that Mickey Mouse is the most popular Disney character with readers. It makes sense that Minnie is in second place, and Pluto is in third. But who would have guessed that Stitch would be a close fourth? That rascal! Rounding out the top five faves is Donald Duck. Who is your favorite? Let us know!

Disney's Hollywood Studios Rules!

It was a close race this year but almost a third of our readers chose Disney's Hollywood Studios as their favorite theme park. Which park is your favorite?

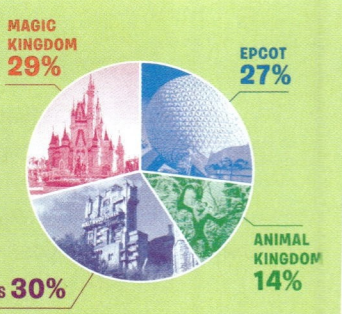

MAGIC KINGDOM 29%

EPCOT 27%

ANIMAL KINGDOM 14%

DISNEY'S HOLLYWOOD STUDIOS 30%

You Love a Wild Ride!

We asked you what types of rides you like best. It turns out most of you like the twists and turns of thrill rides. What daredevils!

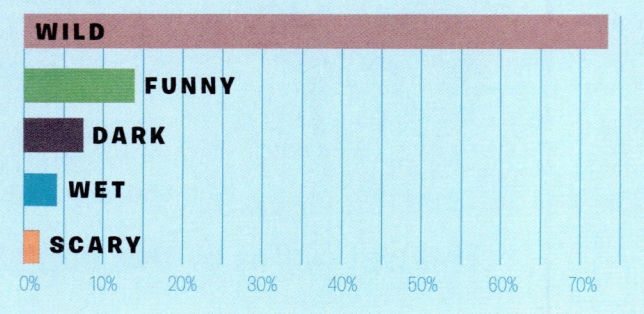

WILD
FUNNY
DARK
WET
SCARY

0% 10% 20% 30% 40% 50% 60% 70%

Look for this Reader Pleaser stamp throughout the book. We've placed it by readers' favorite Disney World shows and attractions. If you'd like to vote for next year's Reader Pleasers, send us a letter or an email and we'll send you a survey form. Use one of the addresses in the orange box below.

READER TIP

Keep an eye out for this sign. Every time you spot one, you will find a great tip sent in by a reader. Do you have any Walt Disney World tips? We would love to hear them!

What Do YOU Think?

Do you agree or disagree with any of the kids in this book? Let us know! First, ask a parent for permission. Together, you can send us a message about your trip. You can write to our email address or send a letter with a self-addressed, stamped envelope to our office. We'll send you a survey and read every one before we write our next book.

Birnbaum's Disney Guides
Kid Expert Applications
Disney Editions
7 Hudson Square
New York, NY 10013

WDI.Birnbaum.Guides.For.Kids@disney.com

READER REVIEW

Every reader who was sent a survey also got an application to be a Birnbaum Ace Reporter. Some of their Reader Reviews appear next to the attraction descriptions in this book. Use the advice from Ace Reporters to decide if an attraction is worth the wait or is one to skip!

AND THE WINNER IS . . .

One lucky Ace Reporter was picked at random to win a Disney prize. And the winner is . . . Benny from Hopkinton, Massachusetts!

Benny is 11 years old. His favorite Walt Disney World attractions are TRON Lightcycle/Run and Guardians of the Galaxy: Cosmic Rewind. Who's on top of his favorite characters list? Mickey Mouse and Donald Duck! Benny enjoys baseball, soccer, and wood-working. He also loves to read, crochet, and play video games. The Magic Kingdom park is on his must-do list. And when it comes to Walt Disney World hotels, he's a big fan of the Contemporary Resort.

Way to go, Benny! Thanks for your valuable input to this edition of *Birnbaum's Walt Disney World For Kids*.

Meet Walt Disney!

Walt came to think of Mickey Mouse as his own son.

Walter Elias Disney was born in Illinois on December 5, 1901 — that's more than one hundred years ago. During his life and for all the years after, Walt Disney's company created famous cartoons, movies, theme parks, books, and toys (plus much more) for everyone to enjoy . . . but how did it all begin?

When Walt was a little boy, he would look up at the sky and imagine the clouds were animals. As the wind pushed a cloud, a pig would turn into a cow. Soon, the cow would become a chicken! It was then that young Walt realized that anything was possible with a little imagination.

But he knew that success would not come from daydreaming alone. Growing up on a farm had taught him the importance of hard work. And it's a good thing, because without Walt's hard work, we would never have met the most famous mouse in the world.

MAGICAL MILESTONES

1901
Walt Disney is born on December 5 in Chicago, Illinois.

1928
Walt creates Mickey Mouse. Mickey stars in the cartoon *Steamboat Willie*.

1937
Walt's animators finish *Snow White and the Seven Dwarfs*, one of the first full-length animated films.

1955
Walt's dream to make a family theme park comes true. Disneyland opens in Anaheim, California.

1971
Walt Disney World (sometimes called WDW) opens near Orlando, Florida.

1975
The first WDW roller coaster opens: Space Mountain!

1982
EPCOT opens at WDW.

A mouse is born

In 1928, Walt created a little cartoon mouse. (Walt almost named him Mortimer Mouse. Luckily, Lilly Disney convinced her husband to name him Mickey Mouse instead!) Mickey's first movie was a black-and-white cartoon called *Steamboat Willie*. It was an instant success. But one hit was not enough for its creator. Walt was always looking for new challenges.

In 1937, his company made one of the first full-length cartoon movies: *Snow White and the Seven Dwarfs*. Walt was very proud that he had made a movie for everyone in the family to enjoy. Family was very important to Walt. Every Saturday, he would do something special with his two daughters. They often went to an amusement park. The kids loved it, but Walt was sad that there weren't any rides for parents. He thought, *I wish there were a place where children and grown-ups could have fun together.*

A dream is a wish your heart makes

Since a place like that did not exist, Walt decided to build it. At first he was going to call it Mickey Mouse Park, but then he named it Disneyland. Disneyland opened in Anaheim,

***Steamboat Willie* was the first talking cartoon ever made.**

California, in 1955. Families traveled from around the world to visit it. Disneyland was so popular that Walt's new dream was to build a bigger park: Disney World. He must have wished upon a star — because his dream came true.

Mickey's birthday is NOVEMBER 18. When is yours?

1983
Tokyo Disneyland opens in the capital city of Japan.

Disney's Hollywood Studios opens at Walt Disney World.
1989

1992
Disneyland Paris opens in France.

Disney's Animal Kingdom opens on Earth Day!
1998

2018
Toy Story Land opens at Disney's Hollywood Studios.

The Studios welcomes a new land — Star Wars: Galaxy's Edge.
2019

2024
Tiana's Bayou Adventure splashes down at the Magic Kingdom!

What a Wonderful World!

Walt Disney loved dreaming up stories to tell and new ways to tell them. After he died, his brother Roy kept one of his biggest dreams alive. He made sure Walt's special "world" was built just the way Walt had imagined it. Roy even insisted that it be called Walt Disney World, so everyone would know it had been his younger brother's dream.

Walt Disney World officially opened in Florida on October 1, 1971. Since then, millions of people have stopped in for a visit. Some people come to Walt Disney World for a day, but most stay a bit longer. There is just so much to see and do — theme parks, water parks, restaurants, and more.

Pick a theme park, any theme park

The most famous part of Walt Disney World is the **Magic Kingdom**. It's home to Cinderella Castle, Space Mountain, and those rascally Pirates of the Caribbean. It is also where you can have an adventure with Peter Pan or Winnie the Pooh. Kids of all ages can't get enough of this happy place. Of course, there are three other Disney theme parks to enjoy.

EPCOT is a place of wonder and discovery. Here you can search for Nemo at The Seas with Nemo and Friends, ride the frosty Frozen Ever

Disney's Animal Kingdom celebrates the beauty of nature and the creatures that live in it. It got off to a roaring start in 1998. The park has what it takes to make any kid's day: an African safari ride with wild animals, a gigantic tree that seems real, a roller coaster adventure with an abominable snowman, and a super stage show inspired by *The Lion King*.

Chill out!

Would you like to cool off on a hot Florida day? You can make a splash at a Disney water park. Between **Typhoon Lagoon** and **Blizzard Beach**, it's almost impossible to stay dry. Each one has slippery slides, tube rides, and some very cool pools.

After attraction, and meet Anna and Elsa. It is also a great place to drive a speedy new car and go on a "world tour." Different countries have shops, restaurants, and attractions inside this park. EPCOT opened in 1982.

Are you a showbiz fan? If so, you will get a big kick out of **Disney's Hollywood Studios** theme park. It's filled with attractions that were inspired by movies and TV shows. You can enter a cartoon world at Mickey and Minnie's Runaway Railway and play in Andy's backyard at Toy Story Land. Guests can fly a spaceship in an area called Star Wars: Galaxy's Edge. And The Twilight Zone Tower of Terror scares everybody silly. Disney's Hollywood Studios opened in 1989.

But wait — there's more! Walt Disney World also has boats, bikes, and even horses to ride. It has hundreds of restaurants, shops, and other places to explore. In fact, no matter how many times you visit, there is always something new to see. Will Walt Disney World ever be finished? Not as long as there is imagination left in the world. And that's exactly how Walt would have wanted it.

Getting Ready to Go

Planning a vacation to Walt Disney World can be lots of fun. But it is not as easy as it sounds. There are so many choices to make! Which parks should you visit? What should you pack in your suitcase? And where can you find your favorite Disney characters?

This book should answer many of your questions and help plan your Disney vacation. Remember: It's never too early to get started!

MAKE A SIMPLE SCHEDULE

Did you know that there are more than 300 shows and attractions at Walt Disney World? It could take weeks to see them all. And most people don't have weeks to spend on vacation. That's why it's important to make a schedule before you leave home. Without it, you might miss some of the rides you want to try the most.

What you will need
Paper, a pencil, and this book!

What to do

1. Write **Magic Kingdom** at the top of a piece of paper.

2. Look at the Magic Kingdom chapter. Every time you see an attraction that sounds like fun, write its name on the paper.

3. When you have finished the chapter, look over your list. Then put a star next to your favorite attractions. These are your "must-sees."

4. Now make a schedule for each of the other theme parks you plan to visit.

5. Don't forget to take your Simple Schedules when you visit the parks!

Learn the Disney Lingo

AUDIO-ANIMATRONICS: Life-like robots, from birds and dinosaurs to movie stars and presidents. They seem real — but they're not.

CAST MEMBER: A Disney worker.

CIRCLE-VISION 360: A movie that surrounds you. The screens form a circle.

GUIDEMAP: A theme park map that also describes attractions, shops, restaurants, and entertainment.

IMAGINEER: A creative person who designs Disney shows and attractions.

MAGICBAND: A wrist band that can serve as a park ticket and WDW hotel room key.

Save Room for Souvenirs

When you pack for your trip, make sure you prepare for the weather. Believe it or not, it gets chilly in Florida, especially in the winter. But the summer can be sizzling hot! It's usually warm during the rest of the year. Layers are a good idea, so you can take something off if you get hot. Remember to pack clothes and shoes that are lightweight and comfortable — since you'll do a lot of walking at the parks. And don't overstuff your suitcase. You may need room for the goodies you gather at Walt Disney World. What else should you bring? That's up to you! Here's a short list to help you get started:

- A sweatshirt or sweater
- Comfy sneakers or shoes
- Hand sanitizer
- Shorts and pants
- Long-sleeved and short-sleeved shirts
- A hat and sunglasses
- A swimsuit
- Pajamas
- Rain poncho
- Sunscreen
- Bug spray

Learn More about Walt Disney World

This book has lots of information, but there's another way to learn about Walt Disney World — the Internet. With a parent's permission you can use the (free) **My Disney Experience** mobile app or website, or visit **www.disneyworld.com**. If you have a question and don't have access to the Internet, write to:

**Walt Disney World
P.O. Box 10000
Lake Buena Vista, FL 32830**

Countdown to Walt Disney World!

Take a look at a calendar. On which day does your Disney vacation begin? Once you find it, count back 10 days — that's the day you can start this special countdown.

To do it, draw a circle around the number for each day as it arrives. Then try the daily activity. Be sure to ask a grown-up for help. You can make up your own special activities, too!

10 DAYS TO GO

Start to plan a Disney party. Choose some of your favorite snacks for the menu. Who is on your guest list?

9 DAYS TILL DISNEY

Get to work on your Magic Kingdom Simple Schedule. (Read page 12 to learn how.) Which attractions do you want to visit first?

8 DAYS LEFT

Draw pictures of Mickey Mouse and place them around your house. Challenge your family to search for Hidden Mickeys!

7 DAYS . . .

Have you finished making your Magic Kingdom schedule yet? It's time to start your EPCOT Simple Schedule. Which attractions do you think sound best?

6 DAYS AND COUNTING

Make some mouse ears! Tape strips of paper to make a loop big enough to fit around your head. Then cut out two circles and tape them to the front of the loop. Make a pair for everyone invited to your party.

5 DAYS MORE

Plan your Disney's Hollywood Studios Simple Schedule. And start packing! (Flip back to page 13 for packing tips.)

4 DAYS TO GO

Get some popcorn and watch a favorite Disney movie with your family. Which flick did you pick? What movie do you want to watch next?

3 DAYS — IT WILL BE SOON

Spend some time on your Animal Kingdom Simple Schedule tonight. Which theme park do you hope to visit first?

2 DAYS — JUST 2!

It's Disney party time! Set the table so it looks festive for your party. Be sure to share your park schedules with your family. Remember to wear your mouse ears!

1 DAY LEFT — YIPPEE!

Don't stay up too late — tomorrow is the BIG DAY!

TODAY IS THE DAY!

Month / Day / Year

You're going to Walt Disney World!

Magic Kingdom

When most people hear the words "Walt Disney World," they think of Cinderella Castle, Space Mountain, and Mickey Mouse. They're all in the Magic Kingdom, along with much more. That is why so many kids say the Magic Kingdom is the most special part of Walt Disney World.

You can spend lots of time exploring its six lands — Main Street, U.S.A., Adventureland, Frontierland, Liberty Square, Fantasyland, and Tomorrowland. This chapter will help you decide which shows and attractions you want to see first. After you read it, flip back to page 12. It lists tips on how to make a simple Magic Kingdom schedule. That way you can organize your park visit and avoid wasting time. If you're lucky, you will get to end the day by watching a fireworks show. That's Disney's way of giving guests a kiss good night.

MAIN STREET, U.S.A.

1 Main Street Vehicles
2 Walt Disney World Railroad Station
3 Town Square Theater

ADVENTURELAND

4 Jungle Cruise
5 Pirates of the Caribbean
6 Swiss Family Treehouse
7 The Enchanted Tiki Room
8 The Magic Carpets of Aladdin

FRONTIERLAND

9 Big Thunder Mountain Railroad
10 Country Bear Musical Jamboree
11 Tom Sawyer Island
12 Tiana's Bayou Adventure
13 Rafts to Tom Sawyer Island
14 Walt Disney World Railroad Station

LIBERTY SQUARE

15 The Hall of Presidents
16 The Haunted Mansion
17 Liberty Square Riverboat

FANTASYLAND

18 Prince Charming Regal Carrousel
19 It's a Small World
20 Mad Tea Party
21 The Many Adventures of Winnie the Pooh
22 Peter Pan's Flight
23 Mickey's PhilharMagic
24 Under the Sea —
Journey of The Little Mermaid
25 Dumbo the Flying Elephant
26 The Barnstormer

(continued)

27 Walt Disney World Railroad Station
28 Seven Dwarfs Mine Train
29 Enchanted Tales with Belle
30 Princess Fairytale Hall

TOMORROWLAND

31 Astro Orbiter
32 Buzz Lightyear's Space Ranger Spin
33 Tomorrowland Speedway
34 Space Mountain
35 Tomorrowland Transit Authority PeopleMover
36 Monsters, Inc. Laugh Floor
37 Walt Disney's Carousel of Progress
38 TRON Lightcycle/Run

Parade Route • • • • • • • • • •

Use this map to plan your visit to the Magic Kingdom!

READER TIP

"You may be able to enter Main Street, U.S.A., before the rest of the park opens for the day!"

— Christina (age 10), Los Angeles, CA

HOT TIP!

Town Square Theater is a great place to meet Mickey Mouse. He is there every day! You can ask him to sign the autograph page at the back of this book. And don't forget your camera. Say cheese!

Main Street, U.S.A.

PHOTO BY JILL SAFRO

Are you ready for some time traveling? You will do a lot of it in the Magic Kingdom. Four out of its six lands send you either back or forward in time. Main Street, U.S.A., is one of those lands. It was made to look like a small American town in the year 1900. (Some of it is based on the town Walt Disney grew up in: Marceline, Missouri.)

There are pretty lamp posts, horse-drawn trolleys, and many other touches that make the street charming. If you look both ways before crossing, you may notice a big difference between this Main Street and a real one: There's a castle at the end of it!

There are no major attractions here, but Main Street is a fun place to be. You can sink your teeth into a fresh-baked cupcake, hop aboard a fire truck, or watch a parade pass by.

Walt Disney World Railroad

Walt Disney loved trains. He even had a miniature one in his backyard that was big enough for him to ride on.

The Magic Kingdom trains are real locomotives that were built nearly a hundred years ago. A full trip takes about 20 minutes, but you can get on or off at any train station (Main Street, U.S.A., Frontierland, or Fantasyland).

What do most kids think about the Magic Kingdom's railroad? They love traveling by train. You get a great view of the park — plus a chance to rest your feet.

READER REVIEW

There's no better cure for sore feet than a trip on the Walt Disney World Railroad. A friendly voice gives you information about the park, and there is a nice breeze. It's great for all ages.

— Emma (age 12), Deerfield, IL

HOT TIP!

Walt Disney's name is written on one of the windows on Main Street, U.S.A. Can you spot it? HINT: It's above The Plaza Restaurant.

HIDDEN MICKEY ALERT!

Look by the railing around the statue of Walt Disney and Mickey Mouse at the end of Main Street — it makes a Mickey shadow!

Main Street Vehicles

The Walt Disney World Railroad isn't the only ride on Main Street, U.S.A. Horse-drawn trolleys, old-fashioned cars, and an antique fire engine make trips up and down the street early in the day.

You can climb aboard any one of these vehicles in Town Square or by Cinderella Castle. Each trip is one-way — you will be asked to hop off after the ride.

The vehicles do not run every day. Stop by City Hall (on Main Street) to get the schedule.

When the horses that pull the trolleys take a break, they can usually be found in the Car Barn. It's near the Emporium shop on Main Street. Stop by to say hello!

Adventureland

A trip to Adventureland is like a visit to a jungle. It has so many plants and trees that Tarzan would feel right at home living here. (Don't bother looking for him. He knows the big treehouse belongs to the Swiss Family Robinson!)

As you can tell from the name of this land, the shows and attractions take you on exciting (and silly) adventures.

HIDDEN MICKEY ALERT!

Keep an eye out for the bathing elephants — a Mickey is carved into the rock behind them.

Jungle Cruise

It's a good thing elephants aren't shy. Otherwise, they might get upset when you watch them take a bath. That's just one of the interesting sights on the Jungle Cruise.

The voyage goes through the jungles of Africa and Asia. Along the way you see life-like zebras, giraffes, lions, hippos, snakes, and crocodiles. Don't worry — the only real animals in the ride are the human beings inside the boat.

The Jungle Cruise is usually very crowded — try to get there early in the morning. It's a good idea to ride during the day, when you can see everything. But if you would like a spookier ride, take the cruise at night.

READER REVIEW

Jungle Cruise is so much fun! The animals look real and the captains are really funny. It's a great attraction for all ages — and a nice break from all those roller coasters.

— Ennio (age 12), Hoover, AL

Pirates of the Caribbean

Dead men tell no tales! That's the warning a pirate gives near the start of this attraction. Don't worry — this classic ride isn't going to hurt you. But there is a small dip and some dark scenes, so be prepared.

The journey takes place in a little boat. After floating through a cave . . . *BOOM!* You're in the middle of a pirate attack! Cannons blast while the song "Yo Ho, Yo Ho, a Pirate's Life for Me" plays in the background.

The pirates and animals look real. But they are Audio-Animatronics figures (kind of like robots). Look for a pirate with his leg hanging over a bridge — the leg is really hairy.

In case you didn't know: This is the attraction that inspired Disney's Pirates of the Caribbean movies. *Arrrrr!*

 **LOUD**  **SCARY**  **DARK**

READER REVIEW

My favorite part of the ride is the lady chasing the pirates with a broom! My 6-year-old brother was afraid of the pirate battle. It's really not that scary, but it might be better for older kids.

— Conor (age 10), Cork, Ireland

HOT TIP!

Do you think you would make a good pirate? Find out by joining a special quest called A Pirate's Adventure — Treasures of the Seven Seas. You will use a map and a magic charm to help find treasure and keep enemies away!

READER REVIEW

I like the Magic Carpets of Aladdin. The ride gives you a great view of Adventureland. And you can cool off when the big camel spits at you!

— Jaiden (age 10), Oregon, WI

HOT TIP!

Some riders can control how high or low the carpet flies. If you want this job, ask to sit in the front row of the carpet.

READER TIP

"Check out Magic Carpets of Aladdin after the fireworks — the line may be shorter then."

— Alex (age 9), Niagara Falls, NY

The Magic Carpets of Aladdin

If a genie offered to grant you some wishes, what would you wish for? To be a prince and win the heart of a princess? Maybe not. But that was Aladdin's wish — and thanks to his funny friend, Genie, his request came true (eventually).

You won't find a real genie at this ride, but you will get to take a high-flying trip on a magic carpet — much like Aladdin and Jasmine did in the movie.

The magic touch

This attraction is a bit like Dumbo the Flying Elephant in Fantasyland — riders use joysticks to control the flight. Also like Dumbo, these magic carpets really soar. Beware of the golden camel. It likes to spit at Magic Kingdom guests!

A whole new world

Kids who visit Adventureland may notice that the area has a special look. The shops and decorations make it look like the busy marketplace of Agrabah from *Aladdin*. You might even see characters from the movie during your visit. They love to pose for photos — so have your camera or mobile phone ready.

Swiss Family Treehouse

Before he wrote a book called *The Swiss Family Robinson*, Johann Wyss and his kids imagined what it would be like for their family to be stranded on an island. Together they came up with lots of crazy adventures for the Robinsons. They survive a shipwreck, fight off pirates, and build the most awesome treehouse in the world.

Walt Disney Productions made a movie based on the book in 1960. The Swiss Family Treehouse in Adventureland looks just like the treehouse in the film. In it, you climb a staircase to many different levels. Each room has lots to see. The tree looks very real, but it is not. It has 300,000 plastic leaves, and concrete roots.

HOT TIP!

The Magic Kingdom is famous for its fireworks shows. And one of the coolest places to watch is from the top of the Swiss Family Treehouse. You can't see all the details from up there, but it's still fun. The treehouse gives you a nice view of Cinderella Castle, too. Be sure to check it out.

HIDDEN MICKEY ALERT!

Find the stone seating area outside the Swiss Family Treehouse. Then look at it very closely. It has two Hidden Mickeys on it!

SUPER SPLASH ZONES

There are lots of ways to make a splash at the Magic Kingdom. In Adventureland, look for a group of tiki statues and a golden camel near Swiss Family Treehouse. They're ready to cool you off with a squirt of water. If that's not enough watery fun, head to Casey Junior Splash and Soak Station in Fantasyland. It's splashy fun for everyone.

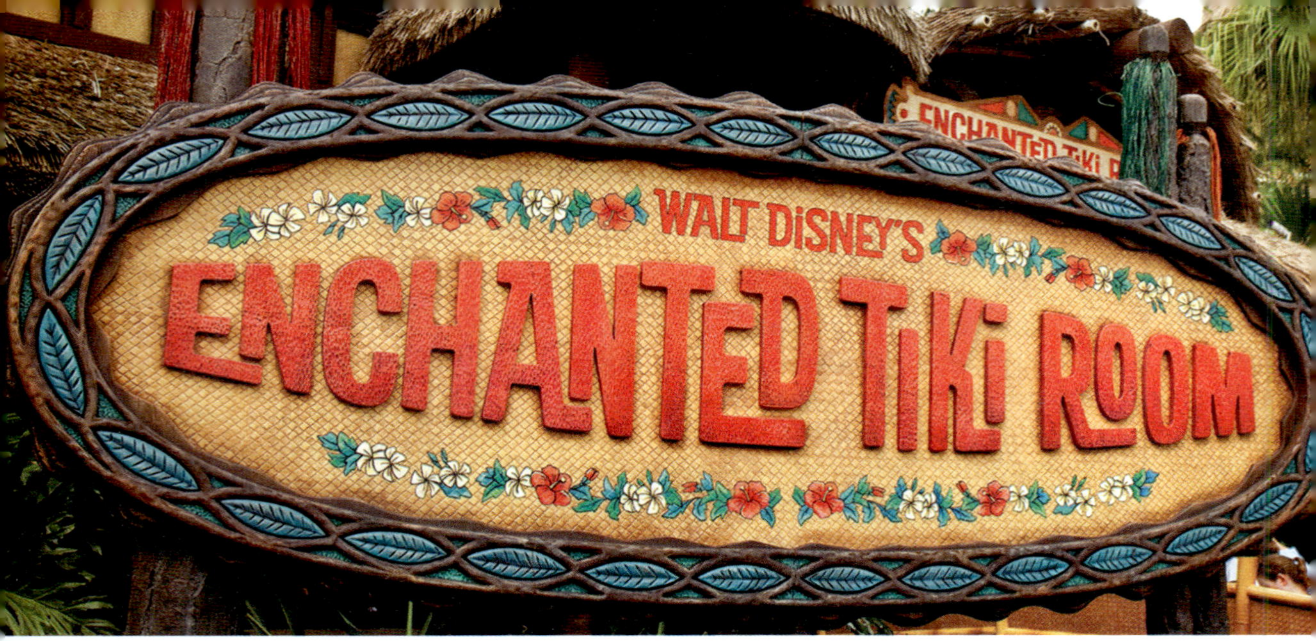

PHOTO BY MIKE CARROLL

HIDDEN MICKEY ALERT!

Look for a Mickey or two on the bird perches inside the Tiki Room.

PHOTO BY MIKE CARROLL

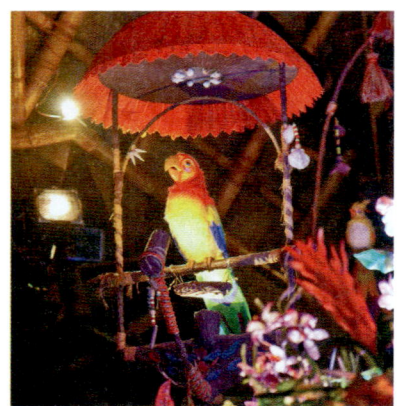

Walt Disney's Enchanted Tiki Room

Birds rule at this attraction. They also sing and crack lots of jokes. If you have been here before, you may know José, Michael, Fritz, and Pierre. They've been singing old favorites like "The Tiki, Tiki, Tiki Room" for 50 years.

So what makes this tiki room enchanted? We already know that the birds all sing — but so do the flowers! In fact, even the totem poles get in on the act. The show happens all around you, so don't forget to look up and behind you. And don't worry — there isn't a bad seat in the house. Be sure to warm up your vocal cords before heading to the Tiki Room — the audience is asked to join in and "sing like the birdies sing." Very small kids may be a little spooked by a thunderstorm.

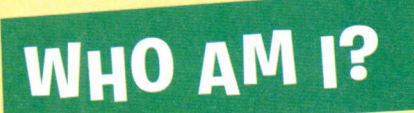

WHO AM I?

- **I am a mouse.**
- **Jaq is my buddy.**
- **My real name is Octavius.**

Answer: Gus

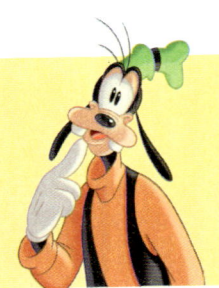

Frontierland

Howdy, pardners! And welcome to the Wild West. Frontierland shows you what America was like when pioneers first settled west of the Mississippi River. It's also where you will find two of the park's wildest rides. Are you feeling brave? You can take a watery trip on Tiana's Bayou Adventure and ride a runaway train at Big Thunder Mountain Railroad. If you'd like something tamer, don't worry. There are lots of ways to have fun in Frontierland.

Tom Sawyer Island

There's only one way to get to Tom Sawyer Island — by raft. That's the way Tom himself used to travel. (Tom Sawyer is a character created by the author Mark Twain.)

Don't expect to find any rides here. In fact, compared to the rest of the Magic Kingdom, it is a pretty calm place. But if you bring your imagination, you can have exciting adventures of your own.

Bouncy bridges and secret exits

The island has a real windmill to wander through, hills to climb, and two bridges. One of them is an old barrel bridge. When one person bounces, everyone does. (Hold on to the ropes if you are worried about falling.)

Across one bridge is a big fort. An Audio-Animatronics blacksmith is working inside it. And there's a secret exit that is really a path through a dark and narrow cave.

In all, there are three caves to explore. They are the best things on the island. Beware: The caves are quite dark and may be a little scary.

Kids love it here

Tom Sawyer Island is fun for everyone. Most kids think the bridges and caves are the best part. Some folks like to bring snacks and have a picnic on the island. There are tables near a place called Aunt Polly's. Tom Sawyer Island may not be open in all of 2026.

READER REVIEW

I think every kid who comes to the Magic Kingdom should explore Tom Sawyer Island. I would have spent more time there if I could. The caves are the best part.

— Dan (age 12), Hummelstown, PA

Tiana's Bayou Adventure

There is a an exciting new ride inside the Magic Kingdom! Tiana's Bayou (say *BUY-oo*) Adventure opened in 2024. Disney Imagineers watched *The Princess and the Frog* movie before they dreamed up the attraction. It gave them lots of ideas for splashy, musical fun. When you ride, you'll hear jazzy tunes. You will see friends from *The Princess and the Frog*. And you'll get wet! There are a few small dips leading up to a giant, watery drop.

You're all wet

No matter which seat you sit in, there's a good chance you will get splashed. But if you sit in the front, you are sure to get soaked. Don't worry, you'll dry off fast in the Florida sun.

The scenery tells the story

The adventure takes guests through scenes based on *The Princess and the Frog*. Watch as fireflies light up the night sky. Listen to Louis share stories about music. And meet Tiana's new pals — a band full of cuddly critters. Try to keep your eyes open during the big drop — it won't be easy.

HOT TIP!

If you sit in the front or on the right side of the log, you get really wet!

 WILD

 SCARY

 WET

YOU MUST BE AT LEAST 40 INCHES TALL TO RIDE TIANA'S BAYOU ADVENTURE.

WHO AM I?

- I live in New Orleans.
- I'm green.
- I love to play the trumpet!

Answer: Louis

Big Thunder Mountain Railroad

Hang on to your hat and glasses, because this is one of the wildest rides in the wilderness. The speedy trains zip in, out, and over a huge, rocky mountain. They pass through scenes with real-looking chickens, goats, donkeys, and more.

The swoops and turns make this a thrilling roller coaster, but it's a bit tamer than Space Mountain. It's a ride you can go on again and again and see new things each time. Look for funny sights in the town — like the poor guy floating around in a bathtub. Try to ride during the day and again at night.

WILD

LOUD

YOU MUST BE AT LEAST 40 INCHES TALL TO RIDE BIG THUNDER MOUNTAIN.

PHOTO BY JILL SAFRO

READER REVIEW

Big Thunder Mountain Railroad is a blast! I really like this attraction because it doesn't have a lot of dips. I think older kids would like it best — the hard turns might shock younger ones. What makes this ride seem very scary is the quick stop it comes to at the end.

— Taylor (age 11), Wyoming, MI

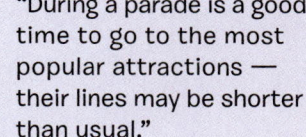
READER TIP

"During a parade is a good time to go to the most popular attractions — their lines may be shorter than usual."

— Joe (age 13), Roanoke, VA

Country Bear Musical Jamboree

You have probably never seen bears quite like these. They sing songs, play musical instruments, and tell jokes. This is a silly show, so go in with a silly attitude. Big Al is one of the most popular bears. And he can't even carry a tune!

The show begins with a new song called "The Country Bear Musical Jamboree." It is performed by a band called Five Bear Rugs. The next song may be familiar to you, especially if you've seen the movie *Zootopia*. Trixie and the girls perform "Try Everything."

Next up is Romeo McGrowl singing "Kiss the Girl" from *The Little Mermaid*. We bet you've never heard it sung quite like this! More Disney tunes follow, all in different country styles. How many songs do you recognize? At the end, all the bears come together for the big finale, which is "The Bare Necessities" from *The Jungle Book*. Kids of all ages enjoy this show.

Frontierland Hoedown Happening

If you're lucky, you'll be in Frontierland for a happy hoedown. (A hoedown is a lively folk dance that includes a lot of people.) In this one, park workers and guests take over the street and show off their dance moves. Disney characters such as the Country Bears may join the fun! The show doesn't run on a schedule — so it's usually a sweet surprse.

Liberty Square

What did America look like in Colonial days? Parts of it looked like Liberty Square. This small area separates Frontierland from Fantasyland. It's a quiet spot with some shops and a couple of popular attractions.

The Haunted Mansion

This haunted house isn't too scary, but there are plenty of ghosts to keep you on your toes. Before you enter, enjoy the interactive wait area and read the funny tombstones outside. (We like the one that says: HERE LIES GOOD OLD FRED. A GREAT BIG ROCK FELL ON HIS HEAD.)

Once inside, you'll be in a room with no windows and no doors. At first, it seems as if there's no way out. It is spooky!

There's a moment before you board a "Doom Buggy" when the room is totally dark. It's just a few seconds, but for some, it's much too long.

The Doom Buggy doesn't move very quickly, but it is still hard to catch all the eerie details. Watch for the door knockers that knock all by themselves, a ghostly teapot pouring tea, and a ghost napping under the table at a party in the ballroom.

READER REVIEW

The Haunted Mansion is spooky at first, but then it is loads of fun. My favorite scene is the waltzing ghosts. Older kids will enjoy this attraction. Younger kids might find this scary. I think it's a very cool ride.

— Will (age 12), Greenville, SC

#13 RIDE Reader Pleaser

DARK

SCARY

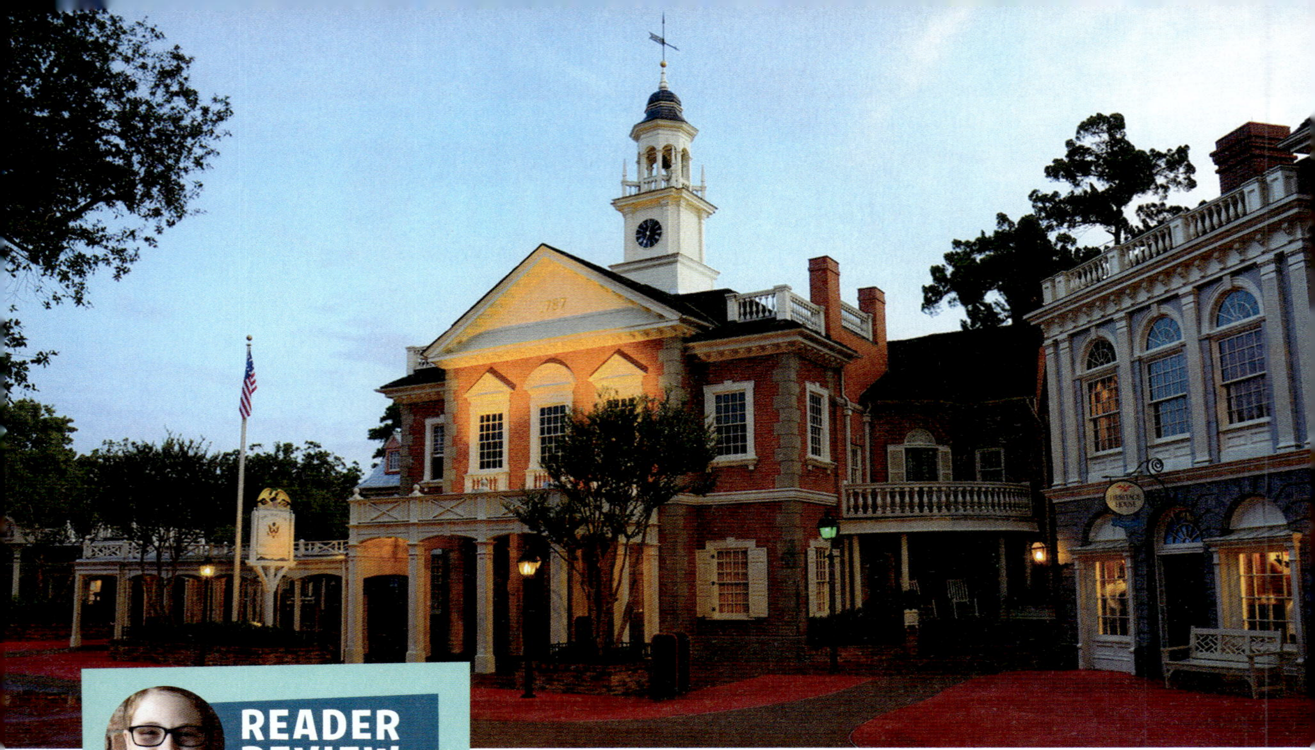

The Hall of Presidents

The first part of this attraction is a film about U.S. history. Then the screen rises and all of the American presidents are onstage together. They are robots called Audio-Animatronics, but they look real. If you watch closely, you will notice the presidents move, nod, and blink.

The attraction is in a building that looks like Independence Hall. (The real Independence Hall is in the city of Philadelphia, Pennsylvania.) Each show is about 22 minutes long.

Liberty Square Riverboat

The *Liberty Belle* riverboat docks in Liberty Square. This big steamboat takes guests on slow, relaxing cruises. It can be a nice break on a busy day (though there aren't many seats). The best spots are right up front or in the back, where you can see both sides of the river as you float along. The 47-foot-tall boat uses steam power. Liberty Square Riverboat may not be open in all of 2026.

Fantasyland

Fantasyland is home to many magical rides that younger kids love. Older kids and even grown-ups enjoy them, too. These attractions are popular, and the waits can be quite long. But the lines are sometimes shorter while people watch a parade or a fireworks show. It's a good idea to skip the parade one day and spend time in Fantasyland. The land may be less crowded late in the day, too.

Prince Charming Regal Carrousel

Most of the attractions at Walt Disney World were dreamed up by Disney Imagineers. But not this carrousel. It was discovered in New Jersey, where it was once part of another amusement park. It was built around 1917.

When you climb on a horse for your ride on the carrousel, be sure to notice that each horse is different. And remember to look up at the ceiling and its hand-painted scenes from *Cinderella*. While you ride, listen for famous Disney tunes, including "When You Wish Upon a Star" and "Be Our Guest."

READER REVIEW

Even though this ride is very short, it is awesome. I love it when you fly through the Goofy sign!

— Samantha (age 8), Chicago, IL

The Barnstormer

One of the wildest rides in Fantasyland is a roller coaster in Storybook Circus. This ride may look small, but it packs plenty of thrills. It takes you on a twisting and turning flight high above the park.

The trip starts out slow, but watch out! Before you know it, you will be soaring through the circus. Hang on tight.

Before you board, be sure to check out the magical area surrounding the ride — that Goofy really is quite goofy.

WILD   SCARY

YOU MUST BE 35 INCHES TALL TO RIDE THE BARNSTORMER.

Mad Tea Party

The idea for the giant teacups that spin through this ride came from a scene in *Alice in Wonderland*. In the story, the Mad Hatter throws himself a tea party to celebrate his un-birthday. That's any day of the year that is not his birthday!

At the Mad Tea Party, you control how fast your cup spins by turning the big wheel in the center. The more you turn, the more you spin. Or you can just sit back and let the cup spin on its own. It may be hard while you are whirling, but try to take a peek at the little mouse that keeps popping out of the big teapot in the center. He is super cute.

READER REVIEW

This ride is fun for the whole family. It's best when everyone helps spin. But if you get dizzy easily, don't turn the wheel, and try not to look outside of your cup as it spins.

— Elizabeth (age 11), Jackson, GA

WILD

Dumbo the Flying Elephant

Just like the star of the movie *Dumbo*, these elephants know how to fly. They would love to take you for a short ride (about two minutes) above Fantasyland. A button lets you control the up-and-down movement of the elephant.

Take your kid brother or sister

Many kids agree that this ride is lots of fun for younger kids. But they all find something to like and think it would be fun to go on with a little brother or sister.

Beware of long lines

Even though Dumbo has doubled in size (so more people can ride), the line for this ride tends to be long. Get there early if you can. If not, you can play in a circus-themed play area while you wait. (A text will let your parents know when it is your time to ride.) If the wait is too long when you get there, try again toward the end of the day. That's when many young kids have already gone home.

PHOTO BY JILL SAFRO

READER REVIEW

I think this ride is more fun if you go on it with your little brother or sister. I like that you can control how high or low you want to be.

— Rachel (age 10), Franklin, TN

HOT TIP!

Need to cool off? Or do you just enjoy jumping in puddles? Head to the Casey Junior Splash and Soak Station. You will be glad you did! (It's not far from the Dumbo ride.)

#20 RIDE Reader Pleaser

READER REVIEW

No matter how many times I go on this ride, it still feels magical! I recommend Peter Pan's Flight for kids of all ages — unless you're afraid of floating in a pirate ship.

— Tiegan (age 12), Minneapolis, MN

HOT TIP!

Would you like to meet some Disney princesses? Head over to Princess Fairytale Hall. Royal folks such as Cinderella and Tiana greet park guests throughout the day. The Hall is in Fantasyland, near the Prince Charming Regal Carrousel.

Peter Pan's Flight

Swoop and soar through scenes that tell the story of how Wendy, Michael, and John get sprinkled with pixie dust and fly off to Never Land with Peter Pan and Tinker Bell. Along the way, you see Princess Tiger Lily, Captain Hook, and Hook's sidekick, Mr. Smee.

Near the beginning of the trip, there's a beautiful scene of London at night. Notice that the cars on the streets really move. Later, watch out for the crocodile that wants to munch on Captain Hook.

When you first board your pirate ship, it seems like you are riding on a track on the ground. Once you get going, the track is above you, so it feels like the ship is really flying.

#17 RIDE Reader Pleaser

DARK

34

It's a Small World

People have a lot in common, no matter where they live. That's the point of this attraction. In it, you take a slow boat ride through several large rooms where singing dolls represent different parts of the world. There are Greek dancers, Japanese kite flyers, Scottish bagpipers, and many more. There's also a cool jungle scene with hippos, giraffes, and monkeys.

All the colorful scenery is set to the song "It's a Small World, After All." The signs at the end say goodbye in different languages. *Aloha! Shalom! Sayonara! Adios!*

READER REVIEW

My grandma and I love this cheerful ride. It has singing dolls and vivid landscapes. No matter what your age — this is a classic attraction that you should not miss.

— Elise (age 12),
Plainfield, IL

#18 RIDE
Reader Pleaser

PHOTO BY JILL SAFRO

HIDDEN MICKEY ALERT!

Many Mickeys can be found in the vines you see in the African scene of It's a Small World.

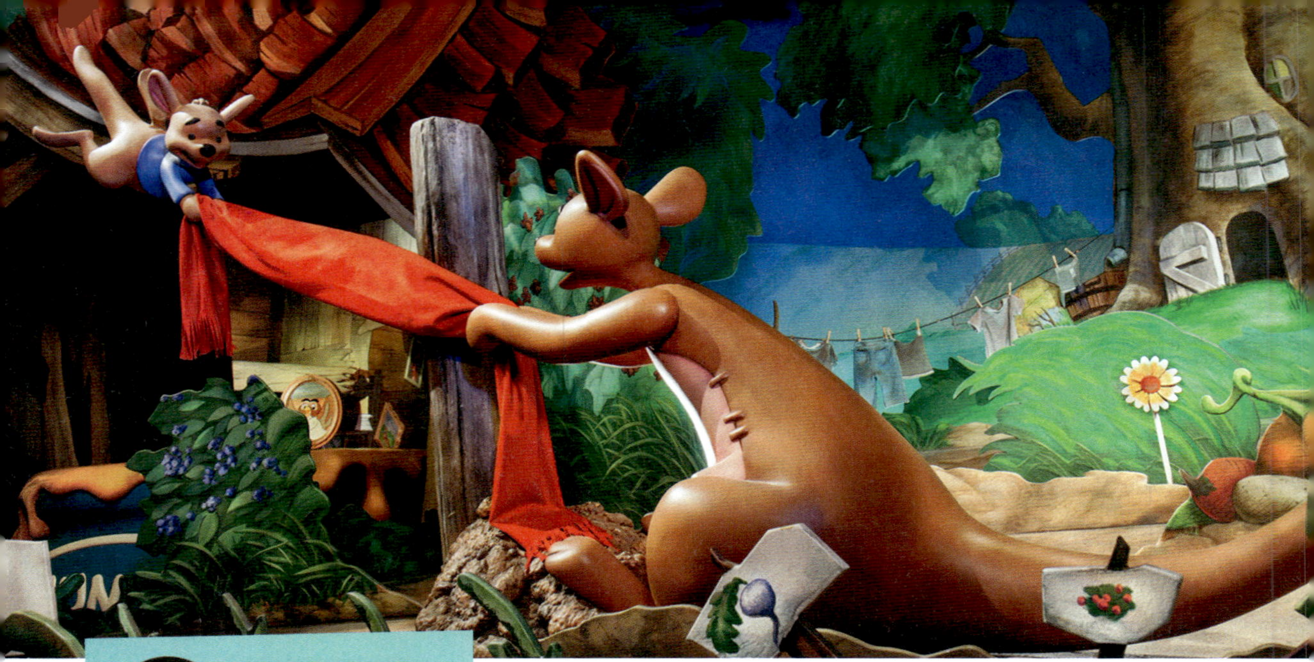

READER REVIEW

My family and I love this ride. My favorite part is when you bounce like Tigger. Get there early because the line can get very long. You don't want to be saying, "Oh, bother."

— Ryan (age 11), Milford, MA

READER TIP

"The games in the waiting area are lots of fun. You can play there even if you don't do the Winnie the Pooh attraction."

— Bobby (age 11), Orlando, FL

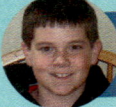

The Many Adventures of Winnie the Pooh

Winnie the Pooh loves his honey. In fact, he will do anything to keep the sweet treat safe. On this trip through the Hundred Acre Wood, see what Pooh must do to rescue his honey pots and his friends, too.

The blustery day

The wind is howling, the leaves are rustling, and everything in Pooh's world is blowing away. Roo and Piglet are up in the air. And Owl's house is about to topple over. Hold on tight, or you just might be swept away next! (Not really.)

A sticky situation

Finally the wind calms and Pooh can get to sleep. But when he wakes up from his silly dream, it's raining. Pooh's honey pots are about to wash away in the flood. He can save them, but will he save himself?

This attraction has an interactive wait area. Some kids think it's almost as much fun as the attraction itself. Be sure to check it out!

Seven Dwarfs Mine Train

Are you ready to visit the mine where a million diamonds shine? Then head to Seven Dwarfs Mine Train! The popular attraction is a roller coaster with a twist — the cars move up and down along the track and they sway a bit from side to side!

Heigh ho, heigh ho!

If you have seen *Snow White and the Seven Dwarfs*, you know where Sleepy, Dopey, Doc, and their friends work — in a diamond mine. At this attraction, guests board train cars and see that colorful mine.

Hang on tight

It's not as speedy as Space Mountain, or as wild as Big Thunder Mountain Railroad, but this ride can spook some kids. If the Barnstormer is too scary for you, skip this coaster.

READER REVIEW

If you are looking for a fun ride, stop here! I love the sharp turns and the big drop. Make sure to see the dwarfs and the gems in the mine. I think this is a great ride for people of all ages. You should go at least twice!

— Gianna (age 10), Au Gres, MI

 #6 RIDE Reader Pleaser

 WILD  SCARY  DARK

YOU MUST BE AT LEAST 38 INCHES TALL TO RIDE SEVEN DWARFS MINE TRAIN.

Under the Sea — Journey of The Little Mermaid

PHOTO BY JILL SAFRO

This attraction invites you to join Ariel for an adventure. Are you ready to dive in? You will go "under the sea" by boarding a special vehicle called a clam-mobile. (They are giant shells, like the ones over at The Seas with Nemo and Friends in EPCOT.) And don't worry about getting wet — the water here is just a cool special effect.

Once you board your clam-mobile, the journey begins. Along the way, you will meet up with Ariel, Flounder, and all of their pals. There is a lot to see and hear in this attraction — you may have to ride it twice to take it all in!

Mickey's PhilharMagic

It's magical. It's musical. It's three-dimensional. It's Mickey's PhilharMagic.

Donald Duck is the real star of this 3-D movie, but it is not a one-duck show. He is joined by his friends Simba, Ariel, Aladdin, Jasmine, Miguel, and, of course, Mickey Mouse.

A one and a two and a three-D

The show takes place in a grand concert hall. Once guests (that's you!) find seats and put on 3-D glasses, it's showtime.

Sit back, relax, and enjoy as the cast of characters show off their musical talents. (Some are more talented than others.) And be sure to keep your eyes and ears open — a whole lot happens at the same time.

Eye-popping 3-D effects take place on the oversize movie screen. Music fills the air. And special surprises happen inside the theater.

What's a PhilharMagic?

In case you were wondering . . . Disney Imagineers made up the word PhilharMagic. They based it on the real word *philharmonic*, which describes a group of musicians who play their instruments at the same time.

READER REVIEW

Wow! Aladdin and Jasmine fly over your head in this amazing attraction. Lots of other characters pop off the screen, too. Put this on your list of shows to see!

— Megan (age 9), Quincy, IL

LOUD   DARK

Enchanted Tales with Belle

Would you like to help Belle tell "the tale as old as time" — the story of *Beauty and the Beast*? You are invited to her dad's cottage to do just that. The fun starts by taking a step through a magical mirror. It transports guests all the way to Beast's castle. There you will meet Madame Wardrobe and her assistant. Together they assign roles to audience members — wave your hand when they ask for volunteers. Once the roles are assigned, guests walk to the library. Expect to be greeted by Lumiere, the candlestick from *Beauty and the Beast*. When Belle arrives, it is story time. This is a popular attraction and the long line moves slowly. Bring something to read while you wait. Belle will be impressed!

READER REVIEW

I like Enchanted Tales with Belle. I got to play a part and help act out the story. I think older kids and younger kids will like it a lot. Plus, you get to take a picture with Belle!

— Emma (age 8), Pleasant Grove, UT

Tomorrowland

Tomorrowland began as a view of the future. As the real world changed, so did this land. Now it's like a city from a science fiction story. The palm trees are made of metal. The rides here let you rocket through space or zoom through the sky. And a famous Space Ranger pops in to visit with guests. A good way to see this land is to ride on the Tomorrowland Transit Authority PeopleMover — it's a relaxing tour and a nice rest for your feet. And even though you won't have a driver's license until the future, you can drive a car in Tomorrowland right now — as long as you are tall enough.

READER REVIEW

I love the fun of riding around Tomorrowland and going through attractions. The turns can be a bit bumpy, but the PeopleMover is mostly relaxing. My dad and I love to look for Hidden Mickeys.

— Sydney (age 10), Leland, NC

Tomorrowland Transit Authority PeopleMover

DARK

This slow-moving ride travels by or through many Tomorrowland attractions. You will even get a peek at Buzz Lightyear's Space Ranger Spin. Pay attention, because you pass by the window very quickly. You will also go through Space Mountain, but you won't see much because it's quite dark.

This ride is a good one to head to when it's hot out. The cars move just fast enough to make a nice breeze. It's interesting to know that the ride doesn't make any pollution. And the wait is usually short. Everybody loves that!

Space Mountain

Thrill seekers head straight for this rocket ride through outer space. It has twists, turns, and a few steep dips. And it all takes place in the dark! Space Mountain is one of the most popular rides in Walt Disney World.

Who turned out the lights?

It's so dark inside Space Mountain that you barely see where you are going. It gets scary — especially if you sit in the front of the rocket. The darkness makes the ride exciting. Every curve comes as a surprise.

You will hear sounds of other rockets zooming around. Of course, the coaster is perfectly safe. The noises are meant to add to the excitement.

Is it too scary?

There's no doubt about it: Space Mountain is scary. But some kids say it's a "good scary." The rockets travel about 28 miles per hour, but it feels much faster.

READER REVIEW

I love the thrill of not knowing where I'm going. I also love that this roller coaster does not have any loop de loops. And it feels like you are really in space!

— Emmy (age 12), McKinney, TX

READER TIP

"For the shortest lines, be there when the park opens!"

— Whitney (age 12), Mount Pleasant, MI

WILD

SCARY

DARK

YOU MUST BE AT LEAST 44 INCHES TALL TO RIDE SPACE MOUNTAIN.

Walt Disney's Carousel of Progress

A lot has changed since the year 1900. Most homes had no electricity, water came from a well, nobody had a TV, and smart phones didn't exist. Life was rough! This attraction shows how American family life has changed since then.

A moving experience

The show is really four short plays. And the performers are all Audio-Animatronics actors. After each scene, the theater moves to the right. That's when you will hear the song "There's a Great, Big, Beautiful Tomorrow." Feel free to sing along.

Walt made it special

Some kids find the show a bit on the slow side, but others think it's quite special. Why? It was introduced to the world by Walt Disney himself. The special event didn't happen at Disney World (it wasn't open yet), but at the World's Fair in New York City in 1964. The attraction has been updated, but the show is still an amusing look at American life. And the Carousel of Progress has made history, too — it has had more performances than any other stage show in the history of American theater.

READER REVIEW

This show is really good. You should go if you like history and technology — which is what it's about. The Audio-Animatronics are amazing! Also, the song "It's a Great Big Beautiful Tomorrow" will get stuck in your head.

— Abby (age 10), Silver Spring, MD

Monsters, Inc. Laugh Floor

Buzz Lightyear has funny neighbors in Tomorrowland — Mike, Roz, and other characters from the movie *Monsters, Inc.* They are all part of a silly attraction that lets you interact with your animated friends. That's right, the audience members not only watch the show — they are a part of it. Don't worry. The monsters don't want to make kids scream the way they did in the movie. This time, they want to make kids laugh. So be ready for lots of wackiness and some very silly jokes!

#16 RIDE Reader Pleaser

 **HOT TIP!**

To get more points on the Buzz Lightyear ride, press the button the whole time and aim at small, moving, or faraway targets.

HIDDEN MICKEY ALERT!

Before you get on the ride, look for a poster that says PLANETS OF THE GALACTIC ALLIANCE. The poster has three Hidden Mickeys on it!

Buzz Lightyear's Space Ranger Spin

In this attraction, everyone is the size of a toy — including you. In fact, you are so small, you fit inside a video game shooting gallery.

To infinity and beyond!

The ride is under the command of Buzz Lightyear. You've just become a Junior Space Ranger, so you are under his command, too. Together, you battle the evil Emperor Zurg.

Zap that Zurg

Zurg and his robots are stealing batteries from other toys. They plan to use the batteries to power their ultimate weapon of destruction. Your job is to fight back. Use the laser cannons in your spaceship to aim at the targets (they look like Z's) and zap Zurg's power. Every time you hit a target, you earn more points. There is a scoreboard next to the laser cannon. It keeps track of all the points you earn.

At the end of the ride, you'll pass a chart. It shows everyone's ranger rank based on their score. Space Ranger Spin may not be open in all of 2026.

READER REVIEW

I love going on this ride! Some kids may be scared, but older kids will probably like it best because it goes up very high and tilts when you reach the top.

— Matthew (age 13), Lakeland, FL

Astro Orbiter

In the middle of Tomorrowland, there is a giant, glowing tower. It is called Rocket Tower. The Astro Orbiter ride is all the way at the top. In it, you soar past colorful planets high above Tomorrowland.

Like on Dumbo the Flying Elephant, you control how high or low your rocket flies. You can ride by yourself or with a friend. (Each rocket fits two people.) But if you want to be the one to control how high you go, be sure to sit in the front.

READER TIP

"If you're afraid of heights, skip Astro Orbiter!"

— Derek (age 13), Spokane, WA

TRON Lightcycle/Run

A powerful new attraction has raced into the Magic Kingdom — TRON Lightcycle/Run. In it, riders zip through a tunnel of flashing lights and zoom along a turbo-charged track. Exciting music and 3-D graphics make this roller coaster very special. And wow is it fast. In fact, it's one of the fastest indoor coasters ever built in a Disney park.

TRON Lightcycle/Run is a big hit with daredevils. But it may be too intense for some kids. Do not eat or drink just before you get there. Each ride lasts about one minute.

DARK

LOUD

SCARY

WILD

YOU MUST BE AT LEAST 48 INCHES TALL TO RIDE TRON LIGHTCYCLE/RUN.

#1 NEW RIDE
Reader Pleaser

#19 RIDE
Reader Pleaser

READER REVIEW

I love this ride. No matter what your age (if you are tall enough), you can drive your parents for once! The race track is nice and long. The line to ride is long, too — but it's worth the wait.

— Lauren (age 12), Harrisburg, PA

READER TIP

"If you get lost at Walt Disney World, don't worry. Just go to the nearest cast member (a worker wearing a name tag) and ask for help."

— Sam (age 9), Eatontown, NJ

Tomorrowland Speedway

You don't need a license to drive around this racetrack (as long as you are at least 32 inches tall and riding with someone at least 54 inches tall). The race cars travel along a rail, but it's not as easy as it looks. Even experts bounce around a bit — and laugh a lot. The race cars are real and are powered by gasoline.

There is something strange about these cars. They don't have any brakes! Just take your foot off the gas pedal and the car comes to a stop.

If you are at least 54 inches tall, you can drive by yourself. If you are between 32 and 54 inches, you're allowed to steer the car — as long as your passenger is at least 54 inches tall. Your passenger can press the gas pedal for you. Don't forget to fasten your seat belt!

Entertainment

The Magic Kingdom is a very entertaining place. It seems like there is always a show starting or a parade going by. Read on to learn about some events that have happened in the park. Which shows will go on during your visit? Ask a parent or guardian to visit *disneyworld.com* to find out. You can expect lots of surprises, too!

Character Cavalcades

Cavalcade (say *KA-vull-kade*) is a fancy way to say parade. And these short parades are quite fancy! In them, Mickey, Minnie, and their pals ride through the Magic Kingdom on colorful floats. What happens if the weather is stormy? Then it's time for the Rainy Day Cavalcade! In it, Disney pals wear boots and raincoats, and sing in the rain. Feel free to splash along.

Pete's Silly Sideshow

There's a special tent in Fantasyland. In it, you can meet silly circus stars—Minnie Magnifique, Daisy Fortuna, The Astounding Donaldo, and The Great Goofini! Yep, Minnie, Daisy, Donald, and Goofy have side jobs at this sideshow. Stop by for some hugs, autographs, and photos with your daring Disney pals. You can ask them to sign the pages at the end of this book.

Let the Magic Begin!

The Magic Kingdom Park welcomes guests with a special show each morning. The fun starts with guests being called to the area in front of Cinderella Castle. Soon Mickey Mouse and his friends come to the stage to welcome you to the park in true Disney fashion. Let the magic begin! Each show lasts about five minutes.

Casey's Corner Piano

If you visit Main Street during the day, you may hear tunes being played on a piano. Some are Disney songs, and others are old-fashioned ones that your parents may know. They'll all make you tap your toes. You'll find the piano player by Casey's Corner restaurant on Main Street, U.S.A.

Disney Starlight

The characters in this nighttime parade sparkle just like the stars in the night sky. Look for favorite friends from *Moana*, *Peter Pan*, *Frozen*, *Coco*, *Wish*, and *Encanto*. This parade happens after dark, so you might have to stay up late to catch it!

Festival of Fantasy Parade

Disney characters star in this afternoon parade. You might even get to meet characters as they pass by. Say hi to Anna and Elsa on the princess float! And don't miss the fire-breathing dragon. It's super cool.

This parade runs in the afternoon and lasts about 12 minutes. Line up early to get a spot on the curb. The show may not happen during stormy weather.

Dapper Dans

The Dapper Dans are a four-person singing group known as a Barbershop Quartet. They entertain guests on Main Street, U.S.A. during the day. Stop in for a show at the barbershop or out on Main Street. They may even perform from their bicycle built for four. That's talent!

Main Street Philharmonic

A marching band makes merry music on Main Street, U.S.A. The band members wear bright red-and-white uniforms, so they are easy to spot. But there is an easier way to find them: Follow your ears!

Mickey's Magical Friendship Faire

Mickey and his pals like to celebrate their friendship with song and dance — and they want you to join them. This musical show takes place in front of Cinderella Castle on most days. In it, Disney friends perform to music from *The Princess and the Frog, Frozen, Tangled*, and other films.

The fun includes appearances by lots of Disney characters — Tiana, Goofy, Donald, Daisy, Prince Naveen, Rapunzel, Flynn Rider, Anna, Elsa, Olaf, Minnie, and Mickey.

Mickey's Magical Friendship Faire takes place on an outdoor stage. It may be canceled if the weather is bad at showtime.

Happily Ever After

There is a happy ending to every day at the Magic Kingdom! This colorful fireworks show takes place high in the sky — up above and all around Cinderella Castle. It captures the heart, humor, and heroism of Disney storytelling.

The show also includes animated projections, laser lights, and merry music. It lasts for about 15 minutes. Don't worry if you can't find space to watch on Main Street — the fireworks can be seen from lots of spots around the park.

Flag Retreat

The Magic Kingdom salutes the spirit of America with a short show each day. It honors the United States of America and the brave people who have protected it. To see the Flag Retreat, go to Town Square on Main Street, U.S.A., at about 5 o'clock. Practice saying The Pledge of Allegiance on your way — it's part of the ceremony. Guests can sing along with the "Star Spangled Banner" as the American flag is lowered. The Flag Retreat lasts about 15 minutes.

Where to Find Characters
at the Magic Kingdom

Disney characters love to greet guests all over the park. A great place to meet Mickey Mouse is Main Street's **Town Square Theater**. Lots of character friends show up on Main Street, U.S.A., throughout the day.

Would you like to see Disney princesses? Go to **Princess Fairytale Hall** in Fantasyland. Minnie Mouse, Daisy Duck, Goofy, and Donald like to hang out at **Pete's Silly Sideshow** in the **Storybook Circus** area of Fantasyland (near the Barnstormer attraction). Elsewhere in Fantasyland you may see Peter Pan, plus Ariel (in her grotto), Winnie the Pooh, Tigger (near The Many Adventures of Winnie the Pooh), and others. Captain Jack Sparrow, Aladdin, and Jasmine may greet guests in **Adventureland**.

When you're in **Tomorrowland**, keep an eye out for Stitch and Buzz Lightyear. Mirabel from *Encanto* greets guests in the **Fairytale Garden** (an area next to Cinderella Castle).

Another way to see favorite Disney pals is at parades and stage shows. Check a park Tip Board for schedules.

The characters love to pose for photos, so have your camera ready. And ask them to sign the autograph pages at the back of this book!

TIPS

 Head to this theme park first, since it has the most rides for kids.

 Try to arrive before the park opens and watch Let the Magic Begin. It's a character-filled show at Cinderella Castle. The show is short but sweet!

You can meet Mickey Mouse in Main Street's Town Square Theater. Use page 150 of this book for his autograph. Don't forget a pen and your camera!

 Want a break from long lines? These attractions usually have short waits: The PeopleMover, Tom Sawyer Island, Enchanted Tiki Room, Carousel of Progress, and The Hall of Presidents.

 Need to cool off on a hot day? Get wet at Casey Junior Splash and Soak Station in Fantasyland. Or hop on the PeopleMover and enjoy the breeze.

 If the Magic Kingdom is open late, it's fun to go on your favorite outdoor attractions after dark.

 There are "chicken exits" in the lines for all scary rides, just in case you change your mind about riding at the last minute.

Do not eat just before riding Astro Orbiter, The Barnstormer, Mad Tea Party, Space Mountain, Seven Dwarfs Mine Train, TRON Lightcycle/Run, or Big Thunder Mountain Railroad.

 If you have never been on a roller coaster, ride The Barnstormer first. If you enjoy it, try Seven Dwarfs Mine Train next — but remember, it is scarier!

 Bring a big pen for characters to use while signing autographs — big pens are easier to grip. They can sign the pages at the back of this book!

Attraction Ratings

COOL
(Check it out!)

- Country Bear Musical Jamboree
- Monsters, Inc. Laugh Floor
- Prince Charming Regal Carrousel
- Swiss Family Treehouse
- Walt Disney's Enchanted Tiki Room
- Liberty Square Riverboat
- Walt Disney's Carousel of Progress
- The Hall of Presidents
- Walt Disney World Railroad

VERY COOL
(Don't miss!)

- Astro Orbiter
- Mad Tea Party
- Jungle Cruise
- Mickey's PhilharMagic
- Dumbo the Flying Elephant
- Enchanted Tales with Belle
- The Magic Carpets of Aladdin
- The Many Adventures of Winnie the Pooh
- Tom Sawyer Island
- The Barnstormer
- Under the Sea — Journey of The Little Mermaid
- Tomorrowland Transit Authority PeopleMover

COOLEST
(See at least twice!)

- TRON Lightcycle/Run
- Tiana's Bayou Adventure
- Big Thunder Mountain Railroad
- The Haunted Mansion
- Peter Pan's Flight
- Buzz Lightyear's Space Ranger Spin
- Pirates of the Caribbean
- Space Mountain
- It's a Small World
- Seven Dwarfs Mine Train
- Tomorrowland Speedway

WHAT DO YOU THINK?

The kids who helped with this book rated all the attractions at Walt Disney World. But your opinion counts, too! If you would like to vote for your favorite attractions, send us a request and we'll send you a survey form. Be sure to get a parent's permission first. We'll use your survey when we create our next book. (Our address is on page 7.)

Where's Mickey?

Disney Imagineers have hidden Mickey Mouse's image all over the Magic Kingdom. Here are a few places to search for Hidden Mickeys while you are in the park. If you would like to meet Mickey in person, go to the Town Square Theater. He visits there every day.

The Haunted Mansion

In the ghost party room, check out the bottom of the long table. There may be a Hidden Mickey made out of saucers and a plate. (It's usually on the left side of the table.)

Carousel of Progress

There are a few Hidden Mickeys in the attraction's Christmas scene. Our favorite is the one on top of the fireplace. It is a Mickey nutcracker! Can you find others?

Tomorrowland Transit Authority PeopleMover

After gliding past Progress City, look to the right. There you will see a woman getting her hair done. What's on her belt? A Hidden Mickey!

Buzz Lightyear's Space Ranger Spin

Once you enter the Buzz building, look for a poster on the right and find the planet called Pollost Prime. One of the continents on the map forms Mickey's profile. And keep your eyes open during the space video scene (about halfway through the ride). You will see this same planet fly by on the right.

It's a Small World

During the ride, pay close attention in the Africa room. If you search the purple leaves on the ceiling, you may spot several Hidden Mickeys. (They are close to the giraffes.)

EPCOT

EPCOT is a great place to make discoveries about the world. At this park, things that used to seem ordinary suddenly become fun. Most of the attractions at EPCOT are in buildings called pavilions (pronounced: *puh-VILL-yuhnz*). The pavilions are spread over four areas of the park — World Celebration, World Nature, World Discovery, and World Showcase. EPCOT's neighborhoods celebrate inventions, ideas, and the wonders of nature. The areas let you explore everything — from the food we eat and your family car to the land, sea, and outer space. (Some details may change in 2026.)

World Showcase lets you travel around the world without leaving the park! There are many different countries to visit here. Each country has copies of its famous buildings, restaurants, and other landmarks. Together, they will make you feel as if you are visiting the real place.

N

WORLD SHOWCASE

WORLD SHOWCASE LAGOON

WORLD DISCOVERY

INTERNATIONAL GATEWAY

DISNEY SKYLINER

WORLD NATURE

WORLD CELEBRATION

ENTRANCE PLAZA

TO BUSES

WORLD CELEBRATION
1 Spaceship Earth
2 Imagination!

WORLD NATURE
3 The Seas
4 The Land
5 Journey of Water, Inspired by *Moana*

WORLD DISCOVERY
6 Test Track
7 Mission: SPACE
8 Guardians of the Galaxy: Cosmic Rewind

WORLD SHOWCASE
9 Showcase Plaza
10 Mexico
11 Norway
12 China
13 Germany
14 Italy
15 The American Adventure
16 Japan
17 Morocco
18 France
19 United Kingdom
20 Canada

Use this map to explore EPCOT.

World Celebration

When you get to EPCOT by monorail, you are in the area called World Celebration. It shows how we connect to each other and to the world around us. The big attraction here is called Spaceship Earth.

Spaceship Earth

You can't miss the silver ball that is the symbol of EPCOT. It's gigantic! The Spaceship Earth ride is inside the big, round building. (The structure is called a geosphere.) The attraction has been around since EPCOT opened in 1982. But the show inside has changed over the years. The story explores human achievements from many years ago up until today. Many folks call Spaceship Earth the Big Golf Ball. Can you guess why?

After the ride, you can spend some time in the "Project Tomorrow" area. It's filled with interactive exhibits.

DARK

READER REVIEW

Some people think this ride is not worth a long wait, but it's one of my family's favorites. It may be a calm ride, but I think it's very interesting. It's a classic!

— Amy (age 12), Clinton, NJ

READER TIP

"The line for Spaceship Earth is usually shortest toward the end of the day!"

— Kersie (age 12), Vancouver, WA

DREAMERS POINT

Walt Disney was a dreamer. And he worked hard to make his dreams come true. One of his dreams was to build a place for grown-ups and kids to have fun together. That dream became Walt Disney World.

Imagineers have created a place for you to dream like Walt. It's a pretty garden called Dreamers Point. The area is filled with plant life and a special statue of Walt Disney. It shows Walt as he dreamed about making EPCOT. You can sit nearby and dream along with him!

Do you have dreams and wishes? Dreamers Point is a great spot to think about making them come true.

IMAGINATION!

This place is a workout for your imagination — the attractions really make you think. There is a ride that tests your creativity and an activity center. Outside, the jumping waters of the Leap Frog Fountains are sure to cool you off. There are a lot of other ways to have fun here, too. Just use your imagination!

Disney and Pixar Short Film Festival

The Magic Eye Theater is a bit unusual — its shows are in 4-D. The films are in 3-D and the theater has special "4-D" effects. Before the action starts, guests watch a pre-show video. In it, Disney and Pixar artists explain how they create animation. As you enter the theater, pick up 3-D glasses. Put them on once you're safely settled in your seat. The first of three short films is called *Get a Horse*. It's a wacky wagon-ride adventure starring Minnie, Mickey, and the rest of the gang. The other movies change from time to time, but they are sure to put a smile on your face. This is a nice place to escape the heat and enjoy animated films.

HOT TIP!

See the attractions inside the Imagination pavilion BEFORE you splash at the Leap Frog Fountains. Otherwise you will be super soggy as you sit through the shows.

Journey Into Imagination with Figment

Think about how different the world would be without imagination in it. There would be no stories to tell, no pictures to draw, and no inventions to make things easier. One thing is for sure — Walt Disney World would not exist!

Imagination is so important to the folks at Disney that they made a special place in EPCOT to learn all about it. It is called the Imagination Institute — and it is having an open house. That means everyone is invited to learn about its projects. And who better to take you on a tour of this special place than Figment himself? (Figment is a purple dragon and host of this attraction. That's him in the picture. You can meet him in the ImageWorks area of the pavilion!)

As you exit the attraction, check out ImageWorks. The play area has hands-on and feet-on activities. Don't miss the "Stepping Tones." They make music when you jump on them.

 LOUD  DARK

LEAP FROG FOUNTAINS

There are lots of places to jump over water at Walt Disney World — hotel pools, lazy rivers at the water parks, and theme park spray zones. But there is a special place where water jumps over you. EPCOT is home to the famous Leap Frog Fountains. Stop by to watch streams of water leap through the air, land with a little splash, then soar again. Kids love to stand under the flying streams of water. Some kids try to catch them! The jumping water is a popular spot for folks to cool off when the weather is warm. You'll find these fountains by the Imagination pavilion.

 ## DID YOU KNOW?

Figment made his first EPCOT appearance in 1983. Where did he come from? The dragon was made by a wizard called Dreamfinder. He collected many interesting items from around the world — tiny wings, yellow eyes, a snout like a crocodile's, childish delight, a bit of purple pigment, and more. When he mixed it all together, he created Figment. Thanks, Dreamfinder!

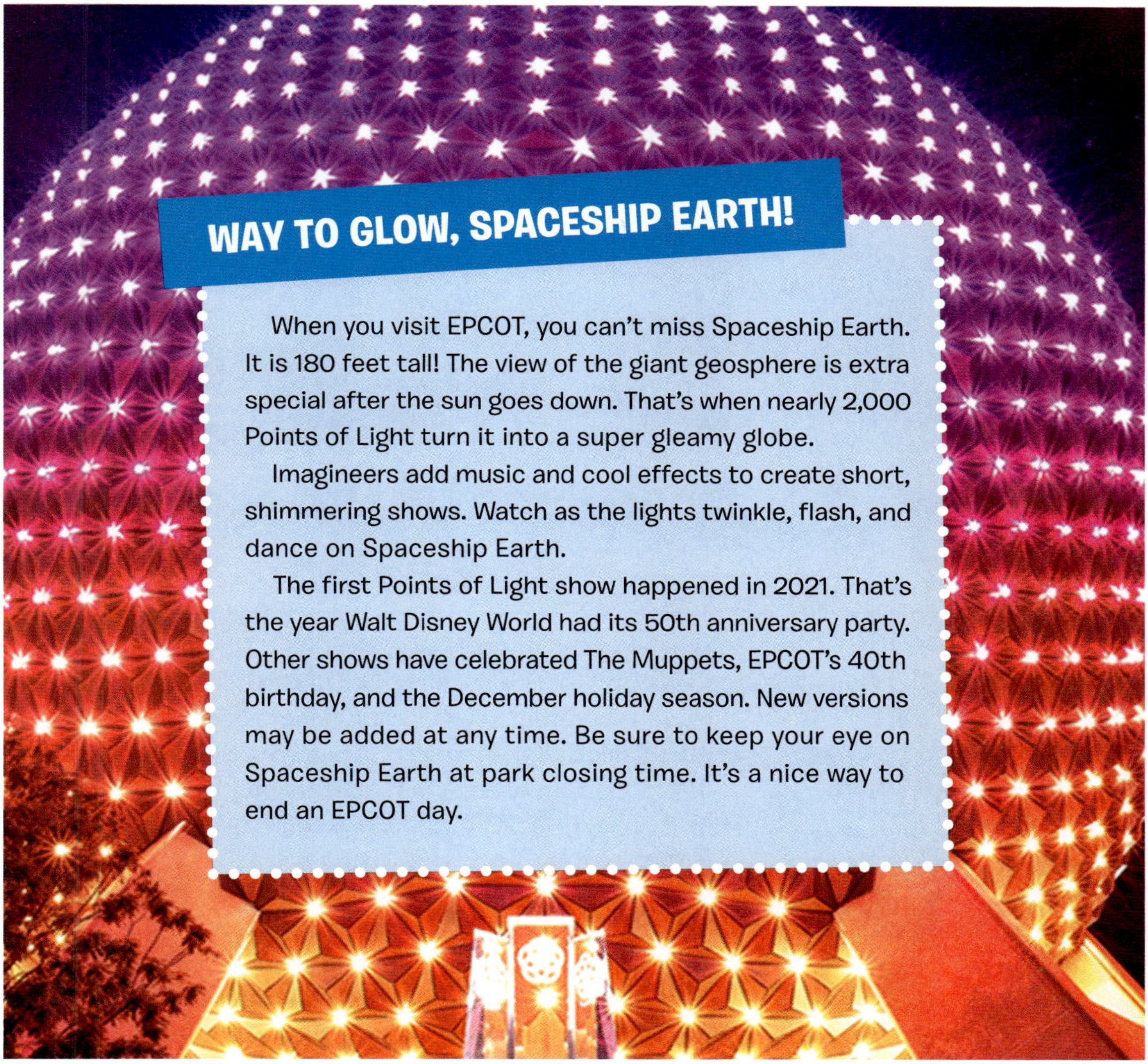

WAY TO GLOW, SPACESHIP EARTH!

When you visit EPCOT, you can't miss Spaceship Earth. It is 180 feet tall! The view of the giant geosphere is extra special after the sun goes down. That's when nearly 2,000 Points of Light turn it into a super gleamy globe.

Imagineers add music and cool effects to create short, shimmering shows. Watch as the lights twinkle, flash, and dance on Spaceship Earth.

The first Points of Light show happened in 2021. That's the year Walt Disney World had its 50th anniversary party. Other shows have celebrated The Muppets, EPCOT's 40th birthday, and the December holiday season. New versions may be added at any time. Be sure to keep your eye on Spaceship Earth at park closing time. It's a nice way to end an EPCOT day.

WHO AM I?

- I live in the ocean.
- I have sharp teeth.
- Fish are my friends – not my food!

Answer: Bruce

World Discovery

SCARY

DARK

WILD

LOUD

#8 RIDE
Reader Pleaser

PHOTO BY JESSICA WARD

Guardians of the Galaxy: Cosmic Rewind

READER REVIEW

Cosmic Rewind is unique and rich with storytelling. You will experience a thrill unlike any other. I think this is the best ride in Walt Disney World!

— Walter (age 9), Southlake, TX

You can zoom through space like Groot, Rocket the Raccoon, and other pals at this thrilling EPCOT attraction. Guardians of the Galaxy: Cosmic Rewind is an indoor roller coaster. It's a very wild ride, but not too scary for daredevils. The experience is different from most roller coasters in one way: The ride vehicles rotate (move in a circle) as they zip along the track. It is very exciting!

If the idea of speeding through dark space on a roller coaster sounds too spooky, or if you get motion sickness, you should skip this ride. And please don't eat just before you go.

Guardians of the Galaxy: Cosmic Rewind is a very popular attraction. Are you tall enough for this wild ride? If you are at least 42 inches tall, the answer is yes!

WHO AM I?

- I'm green.
- I grew up on the planet Zehoberei.
- I'm a Guardian of the Galaxy!

Answer: Gamora

Mission: SPACE

Three . . . two . . . one . . . blast-off! This ride lets you know what it's like to be an astronaut on a trip to outer space. Here, you can take a rocket to Mars or enjoy a trip around Earth.

The Mars voyage is the Orange Mission. It is intense. The orbit around our planet is calmer. It's called the Green Mission.

Each spacecraft holds four guests. Once aboard, it's time for take-off. You will feel the tug of gravity during the Orange Mission launch — just like on a NASA spacecraft. This part lasts nearly a minute, so be ready.

What's your job?

Once you're on your way, things calm down a bit. That may be when you realize you have a job to do. Are you the commander, engineer, pilot, or navigator? That depends on where you sit. It doesn't matter — all the jobs are fun to do. Just before the Orange Mission ends, you will get a strange sensation. It's not weightlessness, but it is definitely out of this world. It's a lot like the feeling astronauts get in outer space.

Mission accomplished

If bouncing or spinning makes you sick, skip the Orange Mission — a lot of people get quite woozy on it. Some feel sick afterward. You can take a cool trip around the Earth, instead — just ask for the Green Mission. Be sure to check the Advanced Training Lab near the Mission SPACE exit. It has activities that most kids enjoy.

READER REVIEW

This is one of the most unusual rides in Disney World. If you're planning to be an astronaut when you grow up, don't miss it. Mission SPACE is a blast!

— Danny (age 12), Chesapeake, VA

LOUD

WILD

DARK

YOU MUST BE AT LEAST 40 INCHES TALL TO RIDE MISSION SPACE.

PHOTO BY JILL SAFRO

READER REVIEW

I was four years old the first time I rode Test Track and I screamed like I never had before! As soon as it was over, I begged to go back on. It was so much fun. It's very fast and thrilling. A great ride.

— Brylee (age 12), McCormick, SC

HOT TIP!

Put long hair in a ponytail before riding Test Track, or it might get all tangled up. And hold on to your hat!

DID YOU KNOW?

The track in Test Track is nearly a mile long. That makes it one of the longest tracks at any Walt Disney World attraction.

Test Track

What is it like to test a brand-new car? You can find out at this attraction—and learn what it's like to make a new car that is as safe as can be.

Where are the brakes?

Test Track is one of Walt Disney World's fastest rides and EPCOT's original thrill ride. As you enter the car, you may notice it does not have brakes or a working steering wheel. Don't worry. It is a self-driving car! And its sound and video equipment let you know what's being tested. You zip around curves, zoom through rooms, and reach a speed of 65 miles per hour.

A crash course in car testing

Kids think this ride is a fun way to learn about cars. Parts of it are loud, so don't be startled if you hear a noisy crash. And remember—the ride is safe. Disney workers tested all the cars. After all, that's what test-driving is all about. After the ride, check out the post-show area.

Disney imagineers recently made big changes at this attraction—so make sure to check out the six special exhibits in the queue area, plus new details throughout the show!

WILD   LOUD   SCARY   DARK

YOU MUST BE AT LEAST 40 INCHES TALL TO RIDE.

World Nature

The Seas

It's easy to find Nemo these days — he is in a building called The Seas with Nemo and Friends! He and his pals can't wait for you to visit. There are more than 2,000 real sea creatures here. There is also a ride, a shark-themed area, and sea-based exhibits to explore.

After taking a quick look at the aquarium, you will enter an area called Sea Base. This is your chance to take a closer look at the creatures and to try the hands-on exhibits. Be sure to visit the Nemo and Friends room, where you can find a real-life version of the little guy. Many kids get a kick out of Bruce's Shark World. (It's a play area where you can learn about sharks.)

The Seas with Nemo and Friends

Jump inside a clam-mobile and let the adventure begin. It's a class trip run by Nemo's teacher, Mr. Ray. It seems little Nemo has wandered off again. Your job is to help find him. Expect to see Dory, Bruce, Chum, Crush, Squirt, and others along the way. And don't worry about Nemo—he won't stay lost for long.

The slow-moving trip under the sea lasts about 6 minutes.

DARK

Turtle Talk with Crush

Everyone seems to love Turtle Talk with Crush. It is a show that lets you talk to the 150-year-old cartoon critter. The best part? He talks back.

The show takes place in a small theater. Grown-ups like to sit on the benches, but most kids prefer the floor in front of the big screen. From the moment Crush swims onto the screen, he has everyone laughing. He asks questions, tells jokes, and makes comments about the different "shells" kids are wearing. He may even talk to YOU! Dory may visit, too. The show lasts about 10 minutes. It's totally awesome, dude!

Bruce's Shark World

Finding Nemo's Bruce the shark has a special play zone in The Seas pavilion. His Shark World has a small maze and a very large version of Bruce himself. It is so big, kids and their families can fit inside! This is a great place to take a picture, so have your camera ready. Bruce's friends Anchor and Chum are on hand for photos, too. Older kids enjoy reading all about sharks and playing games about the mighty creatures.

HOT TIP!

Try to visit the big aquarium at 10 o'clock in the morning or at 3 in the afternoon. That's when the fish get fed. It's fun to watch! (An aquarium is a fish tank.)

JOURNEY OF WATER

Water is the star of the show at this cool nature trail — just like it was in the animated film *Moana*. While guests wander pretty paths they can watch water come to life. It will leap and flow all around them!

EPCOT explorers will learn that water is on an endless journey around the world. And they will find out why the natural water cycle is so important for our planet. Journey of Water is in the World Nature section of EPCOT. Try to visit during the day and again at night. The area is extra beautiful after dark.

THE LAND

The building called The Land looks like a big greenhouse. One of its attractions focuses on food and where it comes from. It's a boat ride called Living with the Land. The other attraction is a high-flying hang glider ride known as Soarin' Around the World. Most kids love it. (Grown-ups do, too!)

Living with the Land

What's the most popular fruit on our planet? The banana! People eat more bananas than any other fruity snack. You will learn lots more food facts on this boat trip. The boat travels through rooms that look like a rainforest, a desert, and a prairie. Then it heads to a greenhouse area.

A recording explains all the things your boat floats past. If you are lucky, you will see some giant vegetables growing here. The greenhouse has produced some of the biggest lemons and eggplants in the world.

In all, The Land grows more than 30 tons of fruit and veggies each year. A lot of it is served to guests in EPCOT restaurants such as the Garden Grill and Coral Reef.

READER REVIEW

Living with the Land is such a cool ride. You get to learn about harvesting fruits and vegetables. It's also very cool to see how Disney is doing its part to help planet Earth.

— Kaylee (age 10), Northford, CT

HIDDEN MICKEY ALERT!

Study the paintings while you wait in line for Living with the Land. One has bubbles on it that connect to form a Mickey head.

Soarin' Around the World

Have you ever wondered what it's like to be a bird? To swoop and soar above the clouds? This attraction lets you do just that. In it, you will fly over natural wonders and famous sites in India, China, Australia, the U.S.A., and more.

Fasten your safety belt

Before the fun starts, you will get a seat in one of the hang gliders. Put your stuff in the basket, fasten your safety belt, sit back, and get ready.

Up, up, and away!

As your glider lifts off the ground, a movie screen lights up in front of you. On it, you'll see many different scenes. You will swoop over oceans, countrysides, and mountaintops. You'll visit sites such as the Eiffel Tower and the Great Wall of China. You may even notice different smells along the way.

Many scenes were filmed using cameras on airplanes and helicopters. Your glider moves the same way those aircraft did — so it seems as if you are really flying.

How real does it feel? Some people lift their feet because they think their toes will hit the items below! The trip takes about five minutes. If you get motion sickness or are afraid of heights, skip Soarin' Around the World.

DARK

YOU MUST BE AT LEAST 40 INCHES TALL TO RIDE SOARIN' AROUND THE WORLD.

READER REVIEW

I love Soarin' because it feels like you're flying. You soar over beautiful views of real places and cute animals. I jumped when the whale popped out of the water! It was unexpected and it made me giggle.

— Avery (age 8), Sloatsburg, NY

Awesome Planet

What is about 4.5 billion years old and home to nearly nine million species of living creatures? The answer is . . . Earth!

You can learn about it in a film called *Awesome Planet*. The 10-minute movie explores the wonders of Earth and its many ecosystems. Some of the ecosystems are in trouble, but there is hope. In fact, there are many ways for us to help our planet. That's pretty awesome.

World Showcase

Anybody can be a world traveler at World Showcase. You can learn about many countries (including the U.S.A.), experience different cultures, and meet people from around the world. You can also take a trip to Arendelle — and even meet Anna and Elsa.

As you visit each country, talk to the folks who work there. Some of the people in each pavilion come from the country they represent. The pavilions were built around a lake called World Showcase Lagoon. If you make the trip all the way around the lake, you'll walk more than one mile!

Canada

If you look at a map of North America, Canada is at the top, just north of the United States. It is a beautiful country. The Canada pavilion at EPCOT is very pretty, too. There's a mountain, a stream, gardens, and a totem pole.

The highlight is a movie called *Canada Far and Wide*. The scenes completely surround you. Since you stand the whole time, it's easy to turn around and see everything. Many kids enjoy the movie but wish the theater had seats.

READER REVIEW

This pavilion shows what Canadians are proud of. I should know — I'm from Canada! I wish the film included even more, but it's a great introduction to my country.

— Shelby (age 14), Calgary, Canada

READER TIP

"There is a walking path and a big waterfall in the back of the Canada pavilion. It's super cool!"

— Judy (age 10), Greenwich, CT

HIDDEN MICKEY ALERT!

Find the totem pole near the front of Canada's Northwest Mercantile. It has two Hidden Mickeys on it! HINT: They are near the top, next to the wings.

United Kingdom

From the city of London to the English countryside, this pavilion gives a varied view of the United Kingdom. Some details to look for include the smoke stains painted on the chimneys to make them appear old, and the grassy roofs that are really made of plastic broom bristles. The buildings look like those in a real British village. Music may be heard in the courtyard. And you may get a chance to meet Alice in Wonderland or Winnie the Pooh.

DUCKTALES WORLD SHOWCASE ADVENTURE

There's treasure to be found in World Showcase — and you can help discover it. It's easy to join Scrooge McDuck, Huey, Dewey, Louie, Donald, Launchpad McQuack, and Webby in their quest to find treasure and solve mysteries — just use the Play Disney Parks app on a mobile device. (Be sure to get a parent's permission first.) The game is fun for kids of all ages. And there's no charge to play!

France

The Eiffel Tower is probably the best-known landmark at the France pavilion. (The real one is in Paris, France.) The buildings look like those in a real French town. Many of the workers here come from France. They speak English with a French accent. Of course, they speak French, too! Surprise them by saying *bonjour* (pronounced: *bohn-zhoor*). It means "good day" in French.

The main attractions — besides the treats at the bakery, an ice cream shop, and a chance to meet Belle — are a *Ratatouille* adventure and films called *Impressions de France* and *Beauty and the Beast* Sing-Along. You can read more about them below.

READER REVIEW

I have been to the real France, and EPCOT's France is just as cool. The food is delicious, especially at the bakery. I think everyone will enjoy the entertainment, shops, and food.

— Ryan (age 12), Pepper Pike, OH

Beauty and the Beast Sing-Along

There are two movies in EPCOT's France pavilion. One is all about the country of France. The other tells the tale as old as time — Beauty and the Beast! This short film makes *Beauty and the Beast* fans very happy. So happy that they may feel like singing.

Spoiler alert: Le Fou played a special role in the *Beauty and the Beast* story — but it wasn't included in the movie. So viewers didn't know what a good guy he really is. This film tells you how Le Fou helped Belle and Beast become friends. Feel free to sing along with the songs in the film. If you don't know the words, don't worry — they appear on the screen. It is shown until about 3 hours before EPCOT closes for the day.

Remy's Ratatouille Adventure

Prepare to be shrunk to the size of a rat in EPCOT's wacky 3-D attraction! After that, you will scurry through Gusteau's Restaurant in a silly adventure. Expect to see characters from the movie *Ratatouille*, plus many interesting sights, sounds, and smells. Hang on! The ride cars twist around a bit — do not ride with a full stomach.

READER REVIEW

This is one of the best rides at EPCOT. Once you put on the 3-D glasses, it feels like you are truly in Gusteau's kitchen. You may even get wet from mop water! This ride is great for all ages.

— Jack (age 13), Grosse Ile, MI

#15 RIDE
Reader Pleaser

LOUD

DARK

Morocco

The country of Morocco is famous for works of art called mosaics (pronounced: *moe-ZAY-iks*). A mosaic is made up of many colorful tiles. That's why there is beautiful tile work on the walls of this pavilion. Moroccan artists made sure the mosaics here were done right.

The buildings are copies of monuments in Moroccan cities, including Fez and Marrakesh. There are shops selling items you might find in the real Morocco. Guests can buy baskets, snacks, jewelry, fez hats, and other clothing. Princess Jasmine visits here, too.

Salam alaikum (pronounced: *sah-LAHM wah-LAY-koom*) means "hello" in Morocco. (It's in the Arabic language.)

HOT TIP!

Talented folks entertain guests all over World Showcase. There is a band in Canada, drummers in Japan, and much more. Which live shows will happen during your visit to EPCOT? Ask a parent to check the My Disney Experience mobile app or website, or *disneyworld.com* to find out.

TOPIARIES

There's something odd about some of the trees and shrubs at Walt Disney World — they are shaped like Disney characters! These plants are called topiaries (pronounced: *TOE-pea-air-eez*). They are carefully grown by gardeners to create their special form. You may spot an Alice topiary by the Mad Tea Party in the Magic Kingdom, Mary Poppins at the Grand Floridian resort, and Pooh and pals in the Crystal Palace restaurant at the Magic Kingdom. In the spring, EPCOT has nearly 80 topiaries on display. How many can you find?

PHOTO BY JILL SAFRO

Japan

The giant temple out front is called a pagoda (pronounced: *puh-GO-dah*). It makes the Japanese pavilion easy to spot. It looks like a famous pagoda in the city of Nara, Japan.

Be sure to notice the evergreen trees. In Japan, they are symbols of eternal life. (Eternal means forever.) Some trees found in traditional Japanese gardens can't survive in Florida. Similar trees were used instead. They like the Florida weather!

Japanese drummers may perform outside the pagoda. The huge department store has lots of souvenirs from Japan. Would you like to say "good morning" in Japanese? Just say *ohayo gozaimasu* (pronounced: *oh-hi-yoh goh-zy-ee-mahs*).

JUST FOR KIDS!

EPCOT has something special for younger kids: Kidcot Fun Stops. There's one in each country at World Showcase — that's 11 in all! At each stop, you can collect activity cards. And you will learn how kids have fun in countries all over the world.

READER TIP

"Try to eat meals early or late in the day to avoid long lines!"

— John (age 14), Washington Township, NJ

READER REVIEW

The American Adventure pavilion is educational yet very entertaining. It is impossible to leave without a smile on your face and a true feeling of pride for being an American.

— Joshua (age 12), Cheektowaga, NY

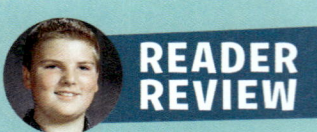

HIDDEN MICKEY ALERT!

As you enter the lobby of The American Adventure, you will see paintings on the walls. One painting shows a wagon being pulled by oxen. There is a Hidden Mickey on the leg of one of the creatures.

The American Adventure

The United States of America is the star of this pavilion. That's why it is called The American Adventure.

The American Adventure show takes place inside a building that looks like Independence Hall (the real Independence Hall is in Philadelphia, Pennsylvania). The show celebrates the American spirit throughout the country's history.

Benjamin Franklin and Mark Twain host the show. (Ben Franklin is one of the founders of the U.S.A. and Mark Twain is one of its best-known authors.) They look so life-like, you may forget that they are mechanical. Ben Franklin even walks up a flight of stairs!

The American Adventure show honors many heroes from history: the Pilgrims, Alexander Graham Bell, Jackie Robinson, Susan B. Anthony, Walt Disney, and others. It's a great way to learn about American history. It's best for older kids.

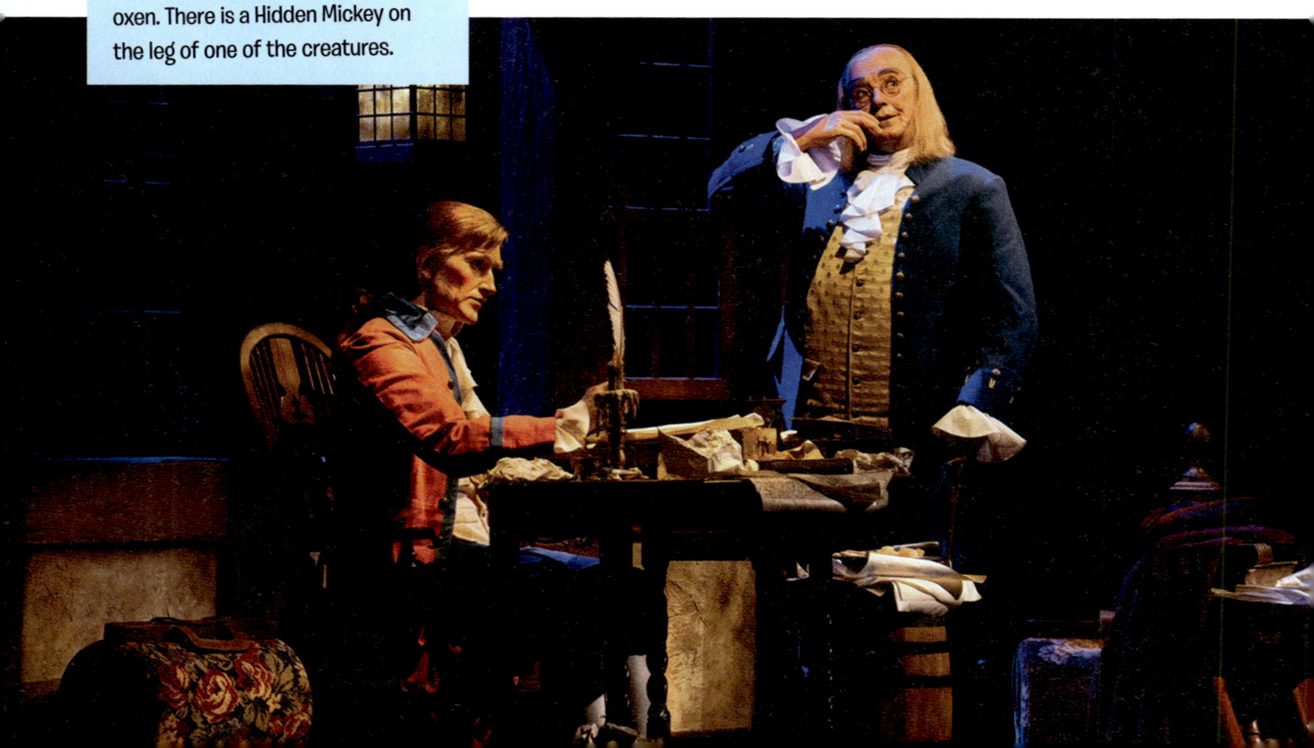

Italy

Venice is an Italian city known for waterways called canals. There are no big canals in EPCOT's Italy, but the pavilion does look a lot like the real thing. The tower is a smaller version of the Campanile, a famous building in Venice.

Take note of the gondolas (pronounced: *GAHN-doe-lahz*) tied to the dock in the lagoon. They are a type of boat used for traveling in the canals of Venice.

Say *buon giorno* (pronounced: *bwon JOR-no*). It means "good day" in Italian.

DID YOU KNOW?

The tallest building in the Italy pavilion is a bell tower. It is 83 feet tall. On top of that tower is a shiny angel statue. It is shiny because it is covered in gold leaf (gold that has been hammered into thin sheets).

INTERNATIONAL MOUSE

Mickey Mouse is famous all over the world. But not everyone knows the movie-star mouse by that name. In Italy he is called Topolino. In Greece he's known as Miky Maoye. Norwegians call him Mikke Mus. In Sweden he goes by Musse Pigg. And in China he's Mi Lao Shu. That's a lot of names for one mouse to remember!

China

READER REVIEW

I really like EPCOT's China. It has a massive gift shop, a pond with fish, and lots of food, plus a movie! I could spend a year — and a lot of money — here.

— Beckie (age 9), Gettysburg, PA

Disney's version of the Temple of Heaven is at the center of this pavilion. It's a landmark in the Chinese city of Beijing. Inside, there is a Circle-Vision 360 movie called *Reflections of China.* (There are no seats in the theater.)

Before going in to the movie, look around the waiting area. It is decorated in shades of red and gold. These colors mean good luck in China.

The film takes guests on a tour of the country. It is worth seeing, but it is more popular with adults than kids. Most younger guests would rather spend their time spying on the fish in the koi pond or checking out the toys inside the big shop.

One way to say "hello" in Chinese is *ni hao* (say: *nee HOW*).

Germany

There isn't a village in Germany quite like the one at EPCOT. It's a combination of cities and small towns from all around the country. Try to stop by the pavilion on the hour so you can see the special cuckoo clock near the toy shop and hear it chime.

In German, "good day" is *guten tag* (say: *GOO-ten tahg*).

READER REVIEW

Germany is one of my favorite pavilions. I love the cuckoo clocks, teddy bears, and sausages. A great time to visit Germany is in October for Oktoberfest. There are special games, food, singing, and dancing.

— Micheline (age 9), Coral Springs, FL

HIDDEN MICKEY ALERT!

You'll find a Mickey in the grass in Germany's miniature village.

Norway

You will discover the history and culture of Norway at this pavilion. The magical land of Arendelle can be discovered, too. Anna and Elsa have a summer home here!

Frozen Ever After

The main building is a castle. It was based on an ancient fortress in Norway's capital city of Oslo. Inside, there is an attraction called Frozen Ever After. On this boat ride, guests travel through the beautiful (and icy) queendom of Arendelle. It includes a Summer Celebration and a visit to Elsa's Ice Palace. Expect to see friends from *Frozen* — including Anna, Elsa, Kristoff, Olaf, and Sven.

Frozen is a popular movie — and this is a very popular attraction. It's fun for guests of all ages. Saying "hello" is easy in Norway. It's *hallo!*

READER REVIEW

This ride is so cool. Literally! I love the part when you drop a bit and go backward. The *Frozen* characters look real! I would recommend this ride for everyone in your family.

— Charlotte (age 10), Pawtucket, RI

MEET ANNA & ELSA

What do Anna and Elsa do when they are not busy building snowmen or preparing for Coronation Day? They greet guests at the Royal Sommerhus in EPCOT's Norway pavilion! Visit their summer home with a camera and autograph book ready. (You can use the pages at the back of this book for autographs.) And the royal sisters are happy to pose for photos.

To find this special spot, look for Norway's wooden church. The Royal Sommerhus is just to the left (on the Mexico side).

Mexico

The pyramid (say: *PEER-uh-mid*) at the Mexico pavilion is home to the Gran Fiesta Tour Starring the Three Caballeros. It is a boat trip that takes you through the country of Mexico.

The Three Caballeros are José, Panchito, and Donald (Duck, that is). They starred in a movie together way back in 1944. Now they are back together and planning to do a big show in Mexico City. But there is a problem. Donald keeps getting lost! Don't worry, there is a happy ending. This is Disney World, after all.

After the ride, you may get to see Donald Duck. He greets guests just outside the pyramid. (Donald moves inside when the weather is rainy.) You may also catch a show by the musical group called Mariachi Cobre. The band plays songs from Latin America.

"Hello" here is *hola* (say: *OH-lah*).

HIDDEN TREASURES OF WORLD SHOWCASE

Attractions like Spaceship Earth and Test Track are easy to find. They're huge! And they are easy to spot on a park map. But EPCOT has more to offer than rides, shows, and attractions. Many World Showcase countries have rooms filled with art, historical items, and other cool treasures. Some galleries are easier to find than others. The one in Japan is in the back of the pavilion. Find it and you will see some of the country's "adorable art."

Have you ever wondered what it's like to live in the desert? Head to Morocco to find out. The American Adventure has a display of American Indian art. And in Norway, you can step inside a Stave Church to learn about Vikings. Older kids like to search for these special spots. How many can you discover?

Items in the galleries change from time to time.

Entertainment

EPCOT is known for its entertainment. There are usually lots of shows and special performances every day. Some entertainment may be different during your visit. Ask a parent to check *disneyworld.com* for updates. Here is a sample of the entertainment at EPCOT.

Meet Disney Friends

EPCOT is a wonderful place to meet Disney characters. You may meet Mickey, Minnie, Pluto, Donald, Goofy, Belle, Mulan, Chip, Dale, Anna, Elsa, Alice, Jasmine, Figment, and others.

Luminous — The Symphony of Us

A special show is presented each night at EPCOT. Luminous has music, lights, fountains, and fireworks. The action takes place on and above a lake called World Showcase Lagoon. You can get a good view from many places around the lagoon. The show is very popular — get there early if you can. It might be canceled if the weather is bad.

Sergio

There is a super silly chef in EPCOT's Italy pavilion. His name is Sergio and he's also a juggler. Sergio doesn't speak — but he loves to blow a noisy whistle while he performs. He juggles with a big soup spoon and a rubber chicken. He may even ask you to join in the fun! Each show lasts about 15 minutes.

World Showcase Performers

There is entertainment at each pavilion in World Showcase. Highlights include drummers in Japan, a rock band at the United Kingdom, folk singers in Mexico, musicians at the Canada Mill Stage, and music in Morocco. There is a funny juggler named Sergio in Italy. A group called The Voices of Liberty sings in The American Adventure pavilion. And rock concerts often take place at the America Gardens Theater near The American Adventure. Arrive early to get a seat.

Jammitors

One of the loudest and wildest shows is inside World Celebration, where musicians bang on trash cans and, sometimes, on one another. It's a blast! (The group becomes the Jammin' Chefs during EPCOT's International Food and Wine Festival — starting in summer and going through most of November.)

Where to Find Characters
at EPCOT

Disney characters love to visit EPCOT. One great place to find them is at CommuniCore Hall in World Celebration. Friends such as Mickey, Minnie, Goofy, and Pluto take turns visiting with guests throughout the day. Figment meets folks in the ImageWorks area of the Imagination pavilion in **World Celebration**. And Moana hangs out by Journey of Water in **World Nature**.

You might also see Disney characters such as Donald Duck, Snow White, Winnie the Pooh, Alice, Mulan, Belle, Jasmine, and Aurora as you wander around the **World Showcase** part of the park. Anna and Elsa are there, too. (The royal sisters have a summer house in EPCOT's Norway and you are invited for a visit.)

Disney characters are always happy to pose for photos. So have your camera ready and say cheese! And don't forget to ask the characters to sign the autograph section of this book.

Details may change in 2026.

TIPS

Start your EPCOT day at Frozen Ever After, then Test Track (if it's open), and Soarin' Around the World. After that, visit Nemo at The Seas with Nemo and Friends. Next, head to the Imagination pavilion.

You can sample different soda flavors at Club Cool. Be sure to go with a parent. A lot of kids think one flavor is yucky. Hint: Its name starts with the letter B.

Need a refreshing splash? Visit the Leap Frog Fountains outside the Imagination pavilion, the squirting sidewalk by Mission: SPACE, or the Journey of Water attraction.

Go to Spaceship Earth later in the day. That is when the line for the attraction is usually the shortest.

Each World Showcase country has an activity card to share. Ask for one at the Kidcot Fun Stop. After you collect the cards, you can keep them in the Magical Memories pages of this book!

Spaceship Earth, Test Track, Mission: SPACE, and Journey Into Imagination with Figment have hands-on activity zones. You can play there even if you skip the attractions.

Bring Disney pins with you so you will have something to trade with cast members (workers) throughout Walt Disney World. Get a parent's permission before you trade anything.

Try not to squeeze the movies at Canada, France, and China into one day. And remember — the theaters in China and Canada don't have seats.

Take time to talk to the people who work in World Showcase. Many of them come from the country of the pavilion they represent — and they have many interesting stories to tell.

At EPCOT, you can visit manatees and watch them gobble up lettuce. Each one eats about 90 pounds of it every day!

Attraction Ratings

COOL
(Check it out!)

- Awesome Planet

- Canada (This pavilion has a movie about Canada.)

- China (This pavilion has a movie about China.)

- Germany

- Japan

- Italy

- Morocco

- United Kingdom

VERY COOL
(Don't miss!)

- The American Adventure (in World Showcase)

- Disney and Pixar Short Film Festival

- France (This pavilion has two films. One is all about France and the other is a *Beauty and the Beast* Sing-Along.)

- Gran Fiesta Tour (in Mexico)

- Journey Into Imagination with Figment

- Journey of Water

- Living with the Land

- Turtle Talk with Crush

COOLEST
(See at least twice!)

- Frozen Ever After (in Norway)

- Guardians of the Galaxy: Cosmic Rewind!

- Luminous — The Symphony of Us

- Mission: SPACE

- Remy's Ratatouille Adventure (in France)

- The Seas with Nemo and Friends

- Soarin' Around the World

- Spaceship Earth

- Test Track

YOUR FAVORITE EPCOT ATTRACTIONS

_____   _____

_____   _____

_____   _____

Disney's Hollywood Studios

Disney's Hollywood Studios park lets you experience imaginary worlds from movies and TV shows. There are attractions that let you ride a Slinky Dog roller coaster, sing along with Anna and Elsa, fly the *Millennium Falcon* spaceship, see how wild stunts are performed, and a whole lot more.

The Studios park looks a little like Hollywood did back in the 1940s. Hollywood is the California city where movie-making got its big start. The Disney's Hollywood Studios park got its big start in 1989. It has shows and attractions based on *Frozen*, *Toy Story*, *Star Wars*, *The Twilight Zone*, Mickey cartoons, and other favorites.

You will also get to see lots of characters, including Mickey, Minnie, Buzz, Woody, Olaf, Vampirina, Chewbacca, and the stars of Disney's newest films and TV shows. Be sure to have your phone or camera ready—there are plenty of surprises in store!

STAR WARS: GALAXY'S EDGE

TOY STORY LAND

N

HOLLYWOOD BLVD.

ECHO LAKE

ANIMATION COURTYARD

SUNSET BLVD.

HOLLYWOOD BOULEVARD
1 Mickey and Minnie's Runaway Railway

ECHO LAKE
2 For the First Time in Forever:
A *Frozen* Sing-Along Celebration
3 Indiana Jones™ Epic Stunt Spectacular
4 Star Tours—The Adventures Continue
5 Mickey Shorts Theater

STAR WARS: GALAXY'S EDGE
6 Star Wars: Rise of the Resistance
7 *Millennium Falcon*: Smugglers Run

TOY STORY LAND
8 Alien Swirling Saucers
9 Slinky Dog Dash
10 Toy Story Mania!

ANIMATION COURTYARD
11 Walt Disney Presents
12 Disney Junior Play and Dance!
13 The Little Mermaid—A Musical Adventure
14 Star Wars Launch Bay

SUNSET BOULEVARD
15 Beauty and the Beast—
Live on Stage
16 Fantasmic!
17 The Twilight Zone™
Tower of Terror
18 Rock 'n' Roller Coaster
19 Disney Villains: Unfairly Ever After

Use this map to explore Disney's Hollywood Studios.

The Twilight Zone™ Tower of Terror

At a height of 199 feet, Tower of Terror is one of the tallest attractions at Walt Disney World. For some park guests, it is also one of the scariest.

Legend says that one Halloween night, lightning hit The Hollywood Tower Hotel. A whole section of the hotel disappeared! So did an elevator carrying five people. No one ever saw them again.

Haunted hotel

Now the hotel is haunted. If you dare to enter it, you are in for a few surprises. First, you walk through a dusty hotel lobby. Then you enter a tiny room, where Rod Serling appears on TV. (He was the host of a spooky show called *The Twilight Zone*.) Once Mr. Serling tells you the story of The Hollywood Tower Hotel, get ready — you are on your way to the Twilight Zone.

Going down!

After waiting in the boiler room, you sit down in a big elevator. The elevator takes you on a short tour of the hotel, where you see some special effects. The highlight is when the elevator cables snap. Whoosh! You plunge down eight floors!

Next, the elevator shoots up to the hotel's 13th floor. It teeters for a moment and then . . . it drops again and again at blazing speed!

WILD

SCARY

DARK

LOUD

YOU MUST BE AT LEAST 40 INCHES TALL TO RIDE TOWER OF TERROR.

READER REVIEW

If you love to be scared out of your mind and taking serious plunges, this ride is for you. In it, you will enter a special elevator and take a quick tour of the hotel. Then the cables snap — and you drop faster than gravity can pull you! Expect the unexpected.

— Benny (age 11), Hopkinton, MA

HOT TIP!

If you need something to hold on to while riding Tower of Terror, grab the handle next to your seat.

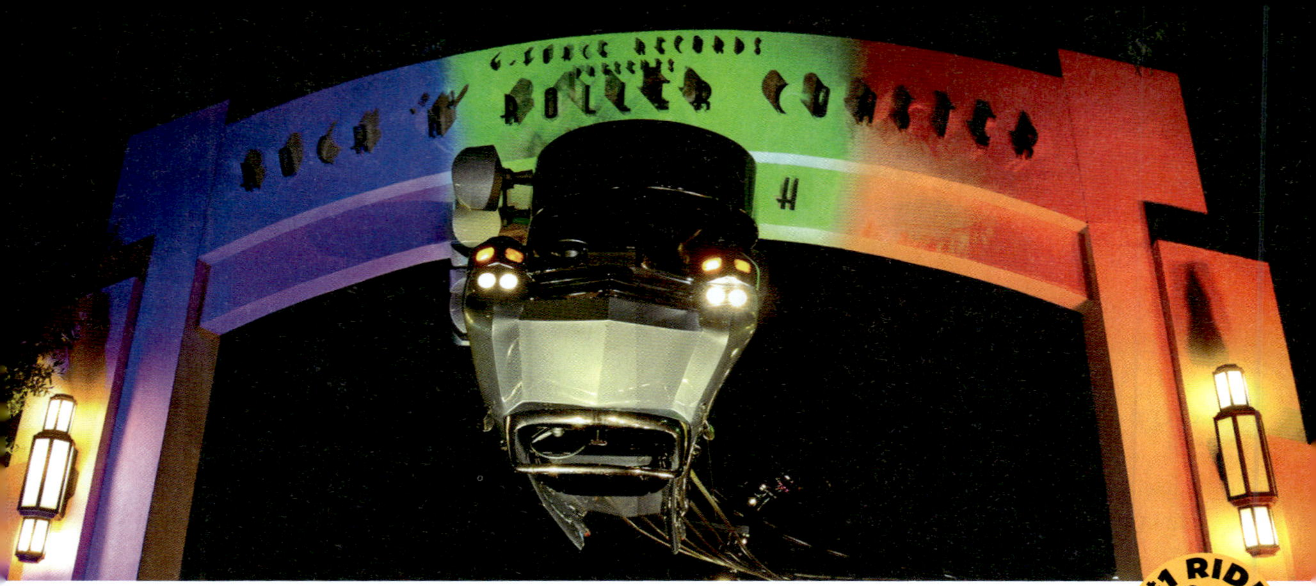

HOT TIP!

Rock 'n' Roller Coaster will soon be getting a new theme. The Muppets are bringing their special wacky energy to Sunset Boulevard! The Electric Mayhem will join up with some awesome musicians for a rockin' music festival. Ask a parent to check *disneyworld.com* for opening dates and details.

Rock 'n' Roller Coaster Starring Aerosmith

This ride rocks. It travels at top speed and flips you upside down! It also has a rock 'n' roll soundtrack that will have you dancing in your seat.

You're invited

Rock 'n' Roller Coaster goes really fast—it takes you from zero to 60 miles per hour in the first three seconds of the ride! You need the speed because you are on your way to an Aerosmith concert—and you are running late.

It's showtime!

The ride takes place in a stretch limousine on a roller coaster track. The limo's radio is tuned to the concert. You can hear the band warming up, but your car is not moving yet. Then, just as the concert starts, the light turns green and you're on your way. You zoom along the California highway and make it just in time for the end of the show. Hang on!

 WILD
 SCARY
 DARK
 LOUD

YOU MUST BE AT LEAST 48 INCHES TALL TO RIDE.

Disney Villains: Unfairly Ever After

Is it possible that Disney villains are not entirely evil? Could it be that they are just misunderstood? That is what this new show is about. The Magic Mirror from *Snow White and the Seven Dwarfs* is the host. He welcomes some of the nastiest villains onstage. Then Cruella De Vil, Captain Hook, and Maleficent will try to convince you and the rest of the audience that they are the most misunderstood. Who will you choose to believe?

PHOTO BY JILL SAFRO

Beauty and the Beast — Live on Stage

It's hard to keep quiet during this stage show—it makes you want to clap and sing along. The music comes straight from Disney's animated film *Beauty and the Beast*.

As the show begins, Belle is frustrated by life in her small town. She is dreaming of exciting, faraway places. Later on, she becomes a prisoner in Beast's castle. All of the castle's residents are under a magic spell. Lumiere, Cogsworth, Mrs. Potts, Chip, and the rest of the gang are there to help (and perform "Be Our Guest"). In the end, the spell is broken. Beast becomes human again.

READER REVIEW

I liked the lively colors and the music in this show. I didn't like how it skipped so fast from one song to the next, because that made it more challenging to follow along, but I still got the story. It's a show the entire family can enjoy!

— Pharra (age 11), Alpharetta, GA

DID YOU KNOW?

The first performance of Beauty and the Beast — Live on Stage took place on November 22, 1991. That was the exact same day Disney's animated version of *Beauty and the Beast* was first shown in United States movie theaters! Have you seen it?

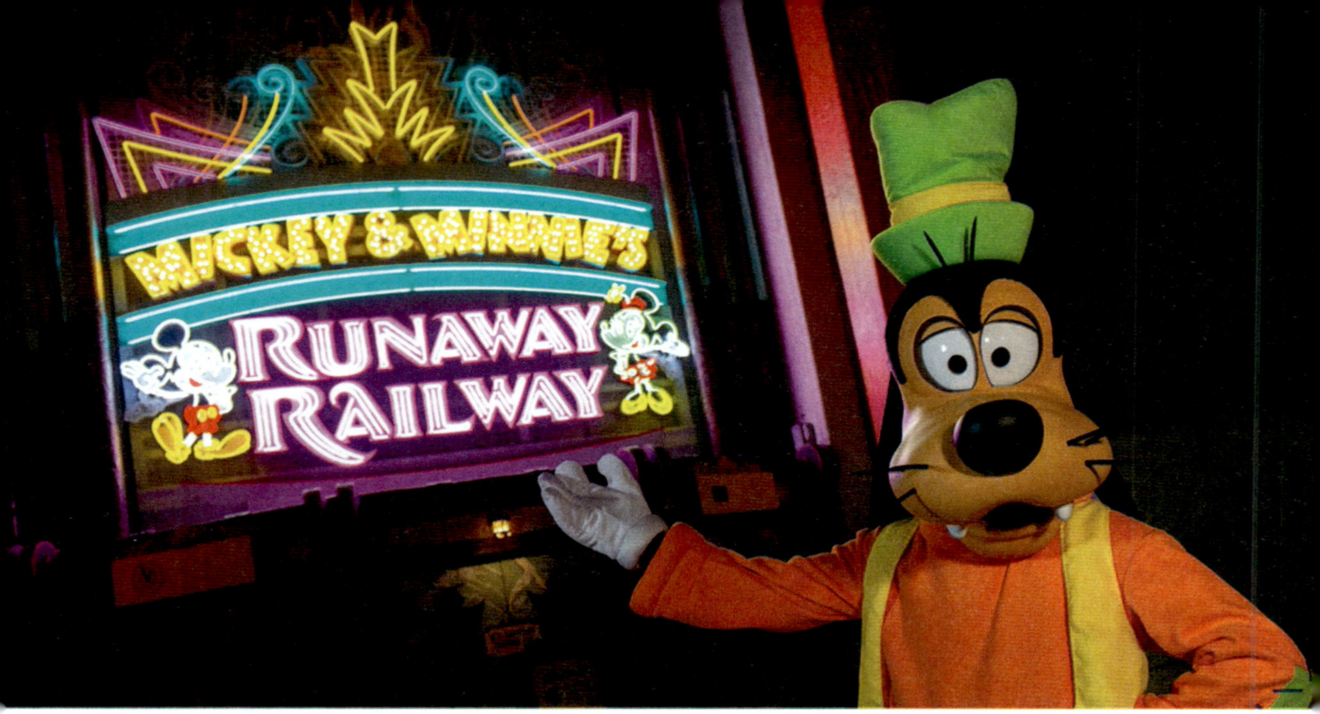

Mickey and Minnie's Runaway Railway

How many cartoons have you seen in your lifetime? Hundreds? Thousands? Well, how many have you actually been IN? Probably not too many! This new attraction puts you in the middle of wild and wacky Mickey Mouse cartoons.

You're a star

At Mickey and Minnie's Runaway Railway, guests walk through a movie screen and become part of the show. Of course, you won't be alone in the crazy cartoon world — lots of Disney friends will join you on the journey.

All aboard!

The adventure begins with Mickey Mouse and Minnie Mouse preparing for a picnic. Then — TOOT! TOOT! A train chugs up and Goofy is the engineer. That's when you join the fun. Anything can happen in the cartoon world, so expect lots of surprises.

WILD

HIDDEN MICKEY ALERT!

Mickey Mouse is one of the famous Hollywood stars whose footprints and handprints are on the sidewalk in front of The Chinese Theatre.

For the First Time in Forever: A Frozen Sing-Along Celebration

Have you ever heard of a song called "Let It Go"? Yes, we thought so! That is just one of the many musical numbers in the movie *Frozen*. And this is the spot to go to if you want to sing along with the characters in the film.

Singing in Arendelle

The experience happens in the Hyperion Theater. The show begins with Arendelle getting two new historians. They tell most of the *Frozen* story in a funny way. When parts of the film play on a giant screen, the audience sings along. Don't know all the words? You can read them on the big screen. Just follow the bouncing snowflake.

Anna and Elsa take the stage!

Singing with the movie is fun, but many kids think the best part is when Anna and Elsa appear live onstage. Anna shows up early, but Elsa arrives a bit later. Don't worry — it's worth the wait.

This show happens several times a day. Ask a parent to check the My Disney Experience app or website for showtimes. And get there a few minutes early. Our *Frozen* friends are quite popular.

WHO AM I?

- I am a starship pilot.
- In France, I'm called Chiktabba.
- I am 8 feet tall and furry.

Answer: Chewbacca

Mickey Shorts Theater

As you probably know, Mickey likes to wear shorts. And if you're a Disney Channel or Disney+ fan, you know that he also stars in them. Short cartoons, that is!

There is a special Mickey cartoon playing at Disney's Hollywood Studios. It's called *Vacation Fun*. And you can have fun watching it at the Mickey Shorts Theater — where the seats look a lot like Mickey's red shorts. The theater is next to an attraction called For the First Time in Forever: A Frozen Sing-Along Celebration.

After watching *Vacation Fun*, you can pose for some silly photos. The photo ops feature some popular Mickey cartoons: *Yodelburg*, *Potatoland*, *Panda-monium*, and more. Say cheese!

WONDERFUL WORLD OF ANIMATION

There is an animated adventure inside the park's Chinese Theater — Mickey and Minnie's Runaway Railway. And there's an animated adventure on the outside, too! It's called Wonderful World of Animation. It takes place on and around the theater.

The 12-minute show sends you through 90 years of Disney and Pixar animation. It is action-packed! The fun begins with a little guy you know well — the one and only Mickey Mouse. All your favorites are included, from *Aladdin* to *Zootopia*. You may have to see it twice to catch it all.

To get a good view, stand in front of the theater. Don't stand right next to a speaker — this show can be loud! And remember: "It all started with a mouse."

Wonderful World of Animation is presented most nights. Will it happen during your visit? Ask a parent to visit *disneyworld.com* to find out.

Disney Junior Play and Dance!

Are you a Disney Junior fan? If so, head straight to this attraction. Friends from Disney Junior programs will dance and sing with you in a stage show. Expect to find favorite characters from shows like *Vampirina*, *The Lion Guard*, and *Doc McStuffins*. Mickey Mouse is there, too!

Have a seat on the floor

As you enter the theater, you may notice something strange — there are no seats. But don't worry. The carpet is comfy, so sit down and make yourself at home. (There are a few benches in the back of the theater. Grown-ups like to sit on them.)

A big hit with little guests

Big kids may get a kick out of Disney Junior Play and Dance, but young kids seem to have the most fun here. If you have little brothers or sisters, take them to this show.

Mickey and Minnie Starring in Red Carpet Dreams

It's no secret that Mickey Mouse and Minnie Mouse are big Hollywood stars. And they have invited you to meet them backstage at Disney's Hollywood Studios — at a special building on Commissary Lane. Inside, Minnie looks like she is ready for a fancy party or awards show. Mickey is decked out in his magical outfit from *Fantasia*. (In that film, he plays the Sorcerer's Apprentice. Say: *SORE-ser-ruhrs UH-pren-tuss.*)

Both mice are happy to greet their fans, pose for photos, and sign autographs — because that's what friendly movie stars do. Check a park Tip Board for their schedule on the day you visit the park.

The Little Mermaid — A Musical Adventure

You don't have to be a fish to have fun underwater — and this new show proves it. In it, you go below the ocean's surface with Ariel and her friends from *The Little Mermaid*. They sing and act out the story on a stage. You will hear musical numbers from the film such as "Part of Your World," "Poor Unfortunate Souls," and "Kiss the Girl." Feel free to sing along!

Beautiful sets and special effects will draw you into the show. Audience members feel like they are part of Ariel's world. To get the best view of the stage, try to sit toward the back of the theater.

This splashy show had its first performance in 2025. It takes place in the Animation Courtyard Theater. The show is fun for guests of all ages.

LOUD

SCARY

DARK

PLAY DISNEY PARKS APP

Play Disney Parks is a free mobile app that can add extra fun to your Disney trip. It has games to play while waiting in lines for shows and attractions. It tests your Disney smarts with trivia questions. And it has games that let you interact with some theme park attractions. You can play with friends and family — but be sure to ask a parent for permission to download the app.

The app offers adventures for all Disney World theme parks. One of the best spots to use it is in Star Wars: Galaxy's Edge. It can translate words written in Aurebesh — the language of the planet Batuu. You'll also be able to find hidden items in the land and hack into droids!

Always ask a parent before you use the Play Disney Parks app. And make sure you have an extra battery pack.

Walt Disney Presents

You probably know a lot about Mickey Mouse — he has a pup named Pluto, he loves red shorts, and Minnie Mouse is his favorite gal. But how much do you know about the man who gave Mickey to the world? You can learn a lot about Walt Disney at this attraction. He is the man who dreamed up Mickey Mouse and The Walt Disney Company.

Take your time

Some of Walt's real belongings are on display here. Look for special items such as Disney family photos, Walt's desk, and the Academy Award he won for *Snow White and the Seven Dwarfs*. Spend time exploring the exhibits before you see the film about Walt.

Fun fact

Did you know that Mickey Mouse wasn't Walt's first famous cartoon character? A rabbit named Oswald was. (That's him below — with his friend Ortensia.) Walt's plans for Oswald didn't quite work out. Luckily, he did not give up, or he never would have created Mickey! To learn more about Walt Disney, turn to page 8.

READER REVIEW

Walt Disney Presents is a wonderful exhibit. It really helps you get to know Walt Disney and the magic that he brought to the world.

— Jennifer (age 12), Salina, KS

PHOTO BY JESSICA WARD

#14 RIDE
Reader Pleaser

READER REVIEW

I love rides and I love arcades — so the combination of the two in Toy Story Mania makes this one of my favorite attractions. I recommend it for older kids and adults.

— Miriam (age 9), Monsey, NY

HOT TIP!

Don't waste too much energy during the practice round at Toy Story Mania! You'll need all your strength for the real games that follow.

Toy Story Mania!

If you think Buzz Lightyear's Space Ranger Spin is a blast, you will love Toy Story Mania! It's like jumping into a life-size video game. It also makes you feel like you're the size of a toy as you travel through colorful rooms and stop in front of screens filled with targets.

This high-tech ride has a twist: All guests wear 3-D glasses. That makes all of the special effects really pop. As you rack up points and trigger surprises, you'll be cheered on by Woody, Buzz, Jessie, Rex, Hamm, and lots of other Toy Story friends.

Toy Story Mania is good for gamers of all ages and skill levels. So if you are a beginner, you'll get better each time you play. In fact, we are pretty sure you will be giving pointers to your parents and grandparents.

Slinky Dog Dash

If you've seen the movie *Toy Story*, you know that Andy is a very creative kid. But did you know he could build a roller coaster? Yep, Andy used his trusty roller coaster kit to build Slinky Dog Dash — a super cool attraction in the park's Toy Story Land.

Andy's creation lets guests ride in a car that looks exactly like Slinky Dog. The cars dash along a brightly colored track that twists around Andy's backyard. This adventure is much tamer than Rock 'n' Roller Coaster, but it's still a ride on the wild side. Guests of all ages enjoy it.

PHOTO BY JILL SAFRO

#10 RIDE
Reader Pleaser

WILD

SCARY

YOU MUST BE AT LEAST 38 INCHES TALL TO RIDE SLINKY DOG DASH.

READER REVIEW

SLINKY DOG DASH IS THE BEST! I love the drops and the thrills. It's definitely wild. It isn't scary, though. Older kids and younger kids will enjoy this ride.

— Evelyn (age 9), Leesburg, VA

Alien Swirling Saucers

Andy won a space-toy playset at the Pizza Planet Arcade — and he wants to share it with you. Just climb inside a rocket-shaped toy and get ready to swirl. The rocket will be pulled by a flying saucer and an alien from *Toy Story*. Don't worry — the Little Green Men are great pilots. (And the rockets do not leave the ground.) While you spin around the galaxy, you will be treated to peppy music and lighting effects.

PHOTO BY JILL SAFRO

LOUD

YOU MUST BE AT LEAST 32 INCHES TALL TO RIDE ALIEN SWIRLING SAUCERS.

LOUD

Indiana Jones Epic Stunt Spectacular

Fire, explosions, daring escapes, and other special effects are the stars of this attraction. Stunt people act out scenes from the movie *Raiders of the Lost Ark* and show how special effects are done. The audience watches from a large theater — and everyone gets a good view of the action.

Fun for everyone

All the surprises keep everyone on the edge of their seats. One of the best parts of the show is the re-creation of a classic movie scene. In it, a giant boulder rolls down and seems to crush Indiana Jones. Even though you know it's a stunt, it seems quite real.

Don't try this at home

Expert stunt people act out the scenes and explain how each of the stunts was done. They make it look easy, but it is not. Don't try this at home!

PHOTO BY JESSICA WARD

WELCOME TO MONSTROPOLIS!

If you make your way over to the area that used to be called Grand Avenue, you might notice that some walls have gone up. This is because Disney Imagineers are working hard on a brand-new area of the park. It will be themed to the Disney•Pixar movie *Monsters, Inc.*

When it opens, guests will be able to enter Monstropolis. You'll even be able to visit the factory where Mike Wazowski and Sulley work! Inside the factory, you will find a scream-worthy roller coaster unlike any other Disney coaster. Why? Because on this coaster, you will hang from the ride's track, just like those closet doors in the movie!

Once you've got your feet back on the ground, you might want to check out the rest of Monstropolis. There will be shopping, restaurants, and a new theater show, too! When will it open? Ask a parent to visit *disneyworld.com* to find out.

WHO AM I?

- I live in a kingdom called Rosas.
- Dahlia is my best friend.
- I made a wish upon a star!

Answer: Asha

Star Tours — The Adventures Continue

If you've ever been to Star Tours before, you should come back soon — it's a little different almost every time. The journey through the galaxy makes guests feel like they are part of a Star Wars movie. Before the trip, put on the special glasses — this adventure is in 3-D. Keep your eye out for Princess Leia, Darth Vader, Yoda, Finn, Din Djarin (from *The Mandalorian*), and BB-8.

It feels real

The ride takes place on a flight simulator — the same type used to train astronauts and pilots. Together, the simulator and movie make it feel like you are really zooming through space.

Hang on tight

The Star Tours adventure has sharp turns and lots of bumpy thrills. Do not eat anything just before you enter the attraction.

WILD

DARK

LOUD

YOU MUST BE AT LEAST 40 INCHES TALL TO RIDE STAR TOURS.

PHOTO BY JESSICA WARD

Meet Olaf at Celebrity Spotlight

PHOTO BY JESSICA WARD

"Hi, everyone! I'm Olaf, and I like warm hugs!" That's how Olaf introduces himself to Anna in the movie *Frozen*. If you would like to introduce yourself to Olaf, here is your chance. Olaf greets guests and gives warm hugs throughout day. He also poses for photos at one of his favorite places — the beach! Don't worry, he won't melt. Elsa gave him his own personal snow flurry. That keeps him frozen!

Olaf cannot sign autographs because his arms are sticks. Instead, he gives out cards with his name on them. Make sure to check a Tip Board for Olaf's schedule when you enter the park. And remember, some people are worth melting for.

 HOT TIP!

The waiting area for Celebrity Spotlight is covered — so you will be protected from the sun while you wait to meet Olaf. But Florida gets super hot in the summer. Keep cool with a water bottle that you can refill.

 WHO AM I?

- I'm a red-beaked hornbill.
- The Pride Lands are my home.
- There are two Z's in my name.

Answer: Zazu

Star Wars Launch Bay

The Launch Bay is a walk-through attraction that celebrates the stories and characters of the Star Wars universe. It is part art gallery, part movie museum, and part character meet-and-greet.

That's no moon — it's a space station!

It can be fun to explore here — especially for Star Wars fans. Some areas are like a museum. In it, guests can see a mini *Death Star*. (It looks like a quiet moon, but it's really a space station built by the evil Galactic Empire!) There's a speeder bike from *Return of the Jedi* and a copy of Rey's speeder from *The Force Awakens*. Visitors have a chance to meet Star Wars characters, too.

Wookiees give the best hugs

If you are a fan of Han Solo's favorite fuzz ball, set a course for the Chewbacca meet-and-greet. You can also meet Darth Vader or BB-8. Darth Vader is a bit scary, but Chewie gives some of the best hugs in the galaxy.

Details may change in 2026.

DID YOU KNOW?

Who worked inside the Launch Bay building long before BB-8, Darth Vader, and other Star Wars characters took it over? Disney animators! For many years, this spot was known as The Magic of Disney Animation. Guests could meet the artists and watch them work. Have you heard of *Mulan*, *Brother Bear*, or *Lilo & Stitch*? All three Disney films were made in this theme park!

PHOTO BY JILL SAFRO

Millennium Falcon: Smugglers Run

Would you like to fly on the fastest ship in the galaxy? This exciting attraction lets you do just that. In it, you'll work with a team to complete a mission. You may get to be the pilot, fire blasters, or prepare the ship for hyperspace.

Hondo is the boss

Hondo Ohnaka is the space pirate viewers first met in *Star Wars: The Clone Wars*. Now he runs smuggling missions on the planet Batuu. And he wants you to work for him!

Do your job

The action takes place on the *Millennium Falcon*. It's a spaceship with room for six crew members. And each one has a job to do. If you do your job well, you will score points. If you bang up the ship, you will lose points — and land on Hondo's naughty list. You don't want that. Good luck!

READER REVIEW

This is a realistic simulator ride where you can fly the *Millennium Falcon!* It's fun even if you have never seen Star Wars. Don't ride if you get motion sickness.

— Thomas (age 11), Northampton, MA

HOT TIP!

Are you a fan of the *Millennium Falcon's* co-pilot, Chewbacca? You can hear Chewbacca react and roar as you ride Smugglers Run! Just ask a cast member to help you unlock "Chewie Mode."

SCARY WILD DARK LOUD

YOU MUST BE AT LEAST 38 INCHES TALL TO RIDE MILLENNIUM FALCON: SMUGGLERS RUN.

Star Wars: Rise of the Resistance

What happens when Star Wars bad guys and good guys end up on the same planet? Well, when that planet is Batuu, a battle breaks out. The First Order and the Resistance are here — and they do NOT get along. When they begin an epic battle, guests like you will be in the middle of the action.

A wild ride

Rise of the Resistance includes fast movement, quick stops, and sharp turns. Don't ride on a full stomach!

May the Force be with you

Will you be captured by the evil First Order? Don't worry. The Force is strong in this park. If you change your mind at the last minute, ask a cast member to point you to an exit.

READER REVIEW

This flight does NOT go as planned. The evil First Order captures you! Don't worry — the Resistance has a plan to help you escape. This is a must-do for Star Wars fans, but it might be scary for younger kids.

— Noah (age 13), Ashburn, VA

 SCARY  WILD  DARK  LOUD

YOU MUST BE AT LEAST 40 INCHES TALL TO RIDE STAR WARS: RISE OF THE RESISTANCE.

WELCOME TO THE PLANET BATUU

There is a world within Walt Disney World — and it is inside Disney's Hollywood Studios. When guests visit Star Wars: Galaxy's Edge, they go to a planet called Batuu (say: *Bah-TOO*).

Batuu is very different from Earth. Many years ago, it was a busy place for traders and explorers. But those days are long gone. Now it is visited by a lot of folks on the wrong side of the law. Space pirates, smugglers, and other criminals love it here. So do people trying to avoid the evil First Order. Are you one of them?

Guests who travel here visit a place called Black Spire Outpost. It has shops, snack spots, and two attractions — Star Wars: Rise of the Resistance and *Millennium Falcon*: Smugglers Run. You may even spot some of your favorite characters (good and bad) from the Star Wars universe.

By the way, nobody says hello on Batuu. They say "bright suns!"

Entertainment

Lights! Camera! Action! There is a lot of entertainment at Disney's Hollywood Studios. Most of it has a TV or movie theme. A few of the best shows are described below. Details may change in 2026.

 DARK  SCARY  LOUD

Fantasmic!

What does Mickey Mouse dream about? You can find out at Fantasmic! It's a nighttime show that combines water, lights, Disney characters, movies, music, and a little magic.

Mickey's dreams are fun to watch — but some are a little scary. (Disney villains turn his dreams into nightmares.) In the end, good wins over evil, and Mickey's dreams are happy once more.

Fantasmic is shown in a theater beside a lake. It's very popular, so be sure to line up at least an hour before showtime. And, if it isn't summer, take a jacket or a sweater — it can get chilly. If you sit near the front, you might get a little bit wet. The lake gets lit on fire, too. It's a cool effect, but it may scare young kids. On what nights is Fantasmic performed? Ask a parent to visit *disneyworld.com* to find out.

Disney Movie Magic

The Chinese Theater is at the end of the park's Hollywood Boulevard (say: *BULL-eh-vard*). It has an awesome attraction inside — Mickey and Minnie's Runaway Railway. It has a cool show on the outside, too. After the sun sets, the front of the theater becomes a big movie screen! Disney Movie Magic is a celebration of Disney films. Catch it if you can.

Green Army Drum Corps

A drum corps is a group of musicians who play drums while they march. And Andy's green army men formed a drum corps in Toy Story Land! The talented soldiers are full of energy. Some kids like to walk behind the Green Army Men as they march through Andy's backyard. The soldiers perform on most days.

Where to Find Characters
at Disney's Hollywood Studios

There are plenty of places to see Disney, Pixar, and Star Wars characters at Disney's Hollywood Studios. You can ask them to sign the autograph pages at the back of this book!

Mickey Mouse and Minnie Mouse greet folks in different rooms at a place called **Mickey and Minnie Starring in Red Carpet Dreams**. You will find everyone's favorite snowman, Olaf, in the **Celebrity Spotlight** building.

Pluto and Disney Junior characters such as Vampirina, Fancy Nancy, and Doc McStuffins may appear in **Animation Courtyard**. Darth Vader, BB-8, and Chewbacca meet guests inside Star Wars Launch Bay. Friends and foes from Star Wars like to walk through **Star Wars: Galaxy's Edge**. Watch out for Stormtroopers!

Jessie, Woody, and Buzz Lightyear may greet park guests in **Toy Story Land**. The Green Army soldiers like to perform in Toy Story Land. The green soldiers may play games, too. To meet pals from Disney-Pixar films, go to Pixar Plaza. (It is near the entrance to Toy Story Land.)

Disney friends are always happy to pose for photos. So have a camera ready and say cheese!

Details may change at any time.

TIPS

 Arrive at Disney's Hollywood Studios before the opening time. The gates often open a few minutes ahead of the scheduled time.

 Some shows may not open until late morning. Check a Tip Board or the My Disney Experience app for show times.

 Do you like to search for Hidden Mickeys? Go to the Mickey and Minnie's Runaway Railway attraction. It has dozens of Hidden Mickeys to discover!

 Some folks think the number 13 is scary. But if the wait time at Tower of Terror is 13 minutes, there is probably a shorter wait — and that's not scary at all!

 There are "chicken exits" at both Tower of Terror and Rock 'n' Roller Coaster, just in case you change your mind at the last minute.

 The front rows at Fantasmic get a little wet. The best seats are in the back at either end of the theater.

 The attractions in Toy Story Land and Star Wars: Galaxy's Edge are popular. Get there early, before the standby lines get super long.

 Don't eat just before riding Rock 'n' Roller Coaster, Slinky Dog Dash, *Millennium Falcon:* Smugglers Run, Star Wars: Rise of the Resistance, Alien Swirling Saucers, Tower of Terror, or Star Tours.

Attraction Ratings

COOL
(Check it out!)

- Meet Olaf . . . at Celebrity Spotlight
- Disney Junior Play and Dance!
- Disney Villains: Unfairly Ever After
- Mickey and Minnie Starring in Red Carpet Dreams
- Walt Disney Presents
- Star Wars Launch Bay
- Mickey Shorts Theater

VERY COOL
(Don't miss!)

- Alien Swirling Saucers
- Beauty and the Beast — Live on Stage
- Fantasmic!
- For the First Time in Forever: A Frozen Sing-Along Celebration
- Wonderful World of Animation
- The Little Mermaid — A Musical Adventure
- Disney Movie Magic
- Indiana Jones Epic Stunt Spectacular

COOLEST
(See at least twice!)

- Mickey and Minnie's Runaway Railway
- Toy Story Mania!
- Slinky Dog Dash
- The Twilight Zone Tower of Terror
- *Millennium Falcon:* Smugglers Run
- Rock 'n' Roller Coaster Starring Aerosmith
- Star Wars: Rise of the Resistance
- Star Tours — The Adventures Continue

YOUR FAVORITE HOLLYWOOD STUDIOS ATTRACTIONS

_____   _____
_____   _____
_____   _____

Disney's Animal Kingdom

Disney's Animal Kingdom celebrates animals of every kind, from lions, tigers, and zebras to giant turtles whose ancestors lived during the time of the dinosaurs. And they're all real! You may get closer to them than you've ever been before. There are flying beasts called banshees, too. They are not real, but they sure seem to be.

Animal Kingdom is a theme park with lots of shows and attractions. Just as in the Magic Kingdom park, there are different "lands" to visit in Disney's Animal Kingdom. The park's major lands are called Discovery Island, Asia, Africa, DinoLand U.S.A., and Pandora — The World of Avatar. (DinoLand will be replaced soon and may not be open in 2026.)

All guests enter the park through The Oasis. It's like a jungle. It has lots of plants and a few wild animals. Take some time to look around. Then cross a bridge to Discovery Island, admire the giant Tree of Life, and decide which land to explore first.

Animal Kingdom is a good place to see Disney characters, too. Who can you meet? Ask a parent to check *disneyworld.com* to find out!

N

AFRICA

ASIA

DISCOVERY ISLAND

THE OASIS

DINOLAND U.S.A.

PANDORA — THE WORLD OF AVATAR

ENTRANCE PLAZA

AFRICA
1. Kilimanjaro Safaris
2. Gorilla Falls Exploration Trail
3. Wildlife Express Train to Rafiki's Planet Watch
4. Rafiki's Planet Watch
5. Festival of the Lion King

DISCOVERY ISLAND
6. Tree of Life
7. Discovery Island Trails
8. Zootopia: Better Zoogether

ASIA
9. Feathered Friends in Flight!
10. Maharajah Jungle Trek
11. Kali River Rapids
12. Expedition Everest

DINOLAND U.S.A.
13. Dinosaur
14. The Boneyard playground
15. Finding Nemo . . . The Big Blue and Beyond!

PANDORA — THE WORLD OF AVATAR
16. Avatar Flight of Passage
17. Na'vi River Journey

What's the best way to see Animal Kingdom? Use this map to help you decide.

Discovery Island

Discovery Island is the gateway to all the other lands in the park. The Tree of Life stands near the center of Discovery Island. If you wander near its roots, you will see different kinds of creatures.

Tree of Life

This human-made tree is 145 feet tall. From far away it looks like any other tree. But when you get up close, you will see that this is not an ordinary tree. It's covered with animals!

Artists have carved 325 animal images into its trunk. In fact, it's called the Tree of Life because it's covered with so many different kinds of animal life. The lion is easy to see. Other animals, such as the ant and dolphin, are a lot harder to spot. How many can you find? Some kids like to use binoculars to peek at the animals. There is another good way to get a close-up view of the Tree of Life. Just take a short walk along the Discovery Island Trail. It leads to the tree's giant trunk.

READER REVIEW

Once inside Animal Kingdom, you can't miss the Tree of Life. Trying to spot all the animals on the tree is nearly impossible! A great place to search for animals is while in line for the attraction inside the tree.

— John (age 14), Washington Township, NJ

PHOTO BY MIKE CARROLL

Zootopia: Better Zoogether

We are willing to bet that you will notice all the animals carved on the outside of the Tree of Life. But did you know that there are a whole lot more animals hanging out *inside* the tree's trunk? If you have seen the movie *Zootopia*, you just might be familiar with some of them. A bunny named Judy Hopps and a fox named Nick Wilde are two of the characters you will see in this new 3-D movie.

Officer Clawhauser

Once you are seated inside the Tree of Life theater, you will be welcomed to the show by Benjamin Clawhauser. Clawhauser is a cheetah who works as a police officer with Judy Hopps. Disney Imagineers have built an Audio-Animatronics figure of Clawhauser to host this show.

Try Everything!

The world of Zootopia is made up of many different environments called ecosystems. (Say *ee-coh-sis-tums*.) There is Sahara Square, the Rainforest District, and Tundratown, plus nine more. You will visit some of these ecosystems in the 3-D movie. You will also hear new music sung by the characters. Go ahead and clap along!

WHO AM I?

- I am super-duper strong.

- My family lives in Colombia.

- I have a cousin named Dolores.

Answer: Luisa

DinoLand U.S.A.

The entrance to this land is marked by a bridge and a dinosaur skeleton. Inside, you may discover life-like dinosaurs and animals that have existed since prehistoric times. The main attraction is called Dinosaur, but there are lots of other things to see and do. DinoLand U.S.A. may not be open in all of 2026. Why? Disney Imagineers are creating new shows and attractions for this area of the park! For updates, ask a parent to visit *disneyworld.com*.

READER REVIEW

The Boneyard is a future archeologist's dream! There are so many things for younger kids to do. Twisty slides, ropes to climb, and dinosaur bones are all waiting to be found.

— Anna (age 9), Verona, WI

The Boneyard

Are you ready to jump into the biggest sandbox you've ever seen? It's here, and it's filled with bones! You can uncover the bones of a mammoth and find clues about how the animal died.

There are also dinosaur footprints that roar when you jump in them and a big xylophone that looks like dinosaur bones. There's a rope maze for climbing and slides to slip down, too. Be sure to check out the Olden-Gate Bridge. It looks like a dinosaur skeleton. The Boneyard may not be open in all of 2026.

HOT TIP!

The xylophone is next to the trunk in The Boneyard playground. Press the bones to make a sound.

READER REVIEW

No more Dinosaur for me! You heard me right — even at my age (10), this ride is too dark, wild, loud, and bumpy. If you like rides like that, you may like Dinosaur. But it is too stressful for me.

— Maria (age 10), Katy, TX

READER TIP

"Dinosaur is very loud and dark, and it really jerks and pulls you around. Some young kids won't like it at all!"

— Julia (age 11), Prairieville, LA

DID YOU KNOW?

The residents of Animal Kingdom and Disney's Animal Kingdom Lodge are very hungry critters. Together, they gobble up about 10,000 pounds of food each day! The meals come from a special group of experts called the Animal Nutrition Team.

Dinosaur

This thrilling and scary ride takes guests back to the last few minutes of the Earth's Cretaceous Period. (That is when the dinosaurs died out.)

Save the dinosaur

The mission on Dinosaur is to save the last iguanodon. You have to brave a meteor shower and one of the largest Audio-Animatronics creatures Disney has ever made. It is a dinosaur called a carnotaurus, and it may be the scariest thing you've ever seen. This monster has the face of a toad, horns like a bull, and squirrel-like arms. It looks like it's alive. The nostrils even move as it breathes. And, boy, can it run. The carnotaurus runs for about 30 feet. Be careful. The creature is not just after the iguanodon — it wants to eat you, too!

An exciting (and scary) ride

Most kids agree that this is a very exciting ride, but one that might not be for everyone. Kids who don't enjoy scary rides can find some tamer dinos in the Boneyard. But for kids who like to be scared, Dinosaur is a must. This attraction may not be open in all of 2026.

 LOUD  SCARY  DARK  WILD

YOU MUST BE AT LEAST 40 INCHES TALL TO RIDE DINOSAUR.

Finding Nemo: The Big Blue . . . and Beyond!

Uh-oh. Nemo has wandered off again. Will he ever learn? We hope not, since this show tells his story in a whole new way—with music. There are peppy tunes to sing along with during the performance — including "The Big Blue World" and "Go with the Flow."

The action takes place in DinoLand's Theater in the Wild. The show happens inside a building, but it seems like it's underwater. You won't get wet, though, since it's all done with special effects.

The show is presented several times each day. It is popular—try to arrive early. The theater is air-conditioned, so you can cool off while Nemo and his friends entertain. The show lasts about 25 minutes.

LOUD

HOT TIP!

Finding Nemo: The Big Blue . . . and Beyond is a popular show. Plan to arrive about 20 minutes early to get a good seat.

READER REVIEW

I don't love stage shows that much — but the fish are pretty neat! Overall, I think Finding Nemo . . . The Big Blue and Beyond is best for Nemo fans.

— Riley (age 12), Dayton, OH

WILDERNESS EXPLORERS

In the movie UP, Russell is a dedicated Wilderness Explorer. He wants to earn as many merit badges as he can. Now you can become a Wilderness Explorer, too. Start by heading to Wilderness Explorer Headquarters at the Oasis bridge. After you take the official pledge, you will get a book that describes different challenges. Complete a challenge to earn a sticker badge! There are about 30 different badges in all. There is no extra charge to become an Animal Kingdom Wilderness Explorer, and the stickers are free. It's fun for the whole family.

TROPICAL AMERICAS COMING SOON

If you visit Disney's Animal Kingdom in 2025-2026, you may notice that some (or all) of DinoLand U.S.A. has gone extinct. That's because Disney Imagineers have dreamed up new themes and attractions for this area of the park. The new land will be called Pueblo Esperanza, and it will have a Tropical Americas theme!

I Hate Snakes!

One new attraction coming to Pueblo Esperanza will star an archaeologist you might have heard of. His name is Indiana Jones, and he likes to go on adventures. Indy is usually searching for something very valuable and rare that has been lost or hidden for many years. This time, he has heard a rumor about a mysterious creature that lives inside a Mayan temple. You will be invited on an expedition with Indy as he explores the temple . . . but will there be booby traps? Or snakes? Indy hates snakes!

Hola, Casita

If you love the movie *Encanto* as much as we do, then get excited! The home of the family Madrigal—the Casita—is coming to Disney's Animal Kingdom. In this new attraction, you can go inside the Casita and explore with Antonio. He has just received his amazing gift and can't wait to use it. You will visit his rainforest room and ride along as he explores his ability to talk to animals. Will Tío Bruno pop up? We certainly can't talk about it! For updates on Pueblo Esperanza and to find out when these new attractions might open, ask a parent to visit *disneyworld.com*.

WHO AM I?

- I'm from the island Motonui.
- I have a little sister named Simea.
- I'm a voyager!

Answer: Moana

Africa

Before creating this land, Disney Imagineers spent months in Africa. They learned all about its plants and animals. When they came home, they created an African forest and a grassland in Florida. And they filled it with hundreds of the same animals they had seen in Africa. Many of the animals in Animal Kingdom came from special parks and zoos around the world. Some of them were born right here! You can see many animals on a safari ride and learn all about them at Rafiki's Planet Watch.

PHOTO BY JILL SAFRO

Kilimanjaro Safaris

In this wild adventure, you ride in a vehicle that is wide open. There's almost nothing between you and the animals. You may see hippos, lions, giraffes, rhinos, elephants, zebras, and more. Some animals may even come up close. But don't worry — dangerous animals can't get near you. It is perfectly safe. Most of the critters are allowed to come and go as they please — so no two safaris are exactly alike. You never know what you will see!

Keep your eyes peeled for beautiful creatures at all times. And have your camera ready. You can take a lot of interesting photos in these parts.

READER REVIEW

Kilimanjaro Safaris lets you see animals that you never thought you would see in person. I saw lions, rhinos, crocodiles, and much more! I like this ride because I want to become a scientist.

— Samuel (age 8), North Chili, NY

Gorilla Falls Exploration Trail

After you take a ride on Kilimanjaro Safaris, go for a walk in the Pangani Forest. This nature trail has a lot to discover. You may come across a grazing zebra or spot some hippos in a watering hole. And you are sure to see hundreds of fish and birds in the aviary. (Say: *AY-vee-air-ee.*)

No binoculars necessary

Pick up a bird guide (in the aviary) and see how many different birds you can spot. Afterward, make a stop at the meerkat exhibit. Some people call it the "Timon exhibit" because he's a meerkat. (There are no Pumbaas here. Meerkats and warthogs don't get along well in real life.)

Snoop on the troop

At the end of the trail, you may see a troop of gorillas. They are usually hiding out or playing on the hills.

It takes about 25 minutes to see everything on this trail.

READER REVIEW

I love to see all the animals on this trail after we ride the safari. I even got to see a baby gorilla.

There are lots of paths to follow — stay close to your adult. This is fun for everyone.

— Zoe (age 7), Birmingham, AL

Rafiki's Planet Watch

A train called the Wildlife Express is the only way to get to Rafiki's Planet Watch. (Hop aboard in Africa.) During the 7-minute ride, you get a peek at the buildings where animals from the safari ride are cared for.

Conservation Station

After a brief train trip, guests walk on a nature trail to reach Conservation Station. Inside, you can watch as veterinarians treat animal patients. You can spy on snakes and tarantulas in the Reptile Room. (Don't worry, the creepy critters are all behind glass!) You can get a nice view of experts preparing meals for hungry critters, and much more.

Lend a helping hand

Rafiki's Planet Watch teaches you all about animals — and what people can do to help them. There are even ways to find out about conservation projects near your home.

Guests can visit with goats and sheep in an area called Affection Section. It is okay to pet them or brush their hair, but feeding is not allowed. Wash your hands after your visit.

HOT TIP!

Rafiki's Planet Watch closes before the rest of the park. Ask a cast member or check the My Disney Experience app for the closing time — and plan to spend at least an hour there.

THE ANIMATION EXPERIENCE

Do you enjoy Disney's animated films? Have you ever wondered how they are made? Now is your chance to find out. Head to Conservation Station for the Animation Experience. It's a class taught by a real Disney animator. In it, you will see how Disney artists study real animals to create characters. And you'll learn how to draw your own version of a popular Disney character. Each class lasts about 25 minutes.

DID YOU KNOW?

Disney's Animal Kingdom is home to more than 2,000 live creatures and about 300 animal species. Quite a few plants live there, too. In fact, the park has more than four million trees, shrubs, flowers, and other plants!

Festival of the Lion King

This is one spectacular musical show. Even if you have the movie memorized, you are in for a few surprises. Many characters from the film are here, but they look a bit different. Most of them are played by humans dressed in colorful costumes.

An action-packed performance

The theater has big stages that look like parade floats. (That's because they were once in a parade at Disneyland.) On one, Simba sits atop Pride Rock. Pumbaa sits on another. Gymnasts dressed like monkeys jump and do tricks.

The mighty jungle

After singers and dancers perform songs from *The Lion King*, it is time for the big finish. Stilt walkers, acrobats, and dancers join Timon for the song "The Lion Sleeps Tonight." Even the audience gets in on the act, so get ready to clap and sing!

READER REVIEW

The Festival of the Lion King is toe-tapping, sing-along fun for all ages. And there are acrobatics aplenty. Enjoy the show!

— Erin (age 10), Weippe, ID

LOUD

WHO AM I?

- I am a fish.
- I'm blue.
- I speak whale!

Answer: Dory

Asia

Asia is the largest continent on Earth. It's almost twice as big as North America! The land called Asia in Animal Kingdom is a lot smaller than the real thing, but it gives you an idea of what the Asian continent is like. It has jungles and rainforests and amazing animals. It's also home to a raging river. You can whirl down the river on a raft ride called Kali River Rapids. For one of the most exciting experiences of all, ride Expedition Everest. And check out an awesome bird show. It's a real hoot!

Maharajah Jungle Trek

Put on your walking shoes and keep your eyes open. This trail is the place to spot scaly critters called Komodo dragons, plus deer, giant fruit bats (they eat melon), and tigers. You'll also see colorful birds along the way and tons of plants and trees. Check the map at the trail's entrance to know what to look for.

You see the bats about halfway through your walk. Their wings are enormous! In some places, there is no glass between you and the bats. Don't worry — they're not interested in humans. Still, it might be creepy to stand so close to them. If the bats make you uncomfortable, there's a window outside the building that lets you watch them from a distance.

PHOTO BY JILL SAFRO

HIDDEN MICKEY ALERT!

When you visit the Maharajah Jungle Trek, look for wall art near the tigers. You'll find Hidden Mickeys on it!

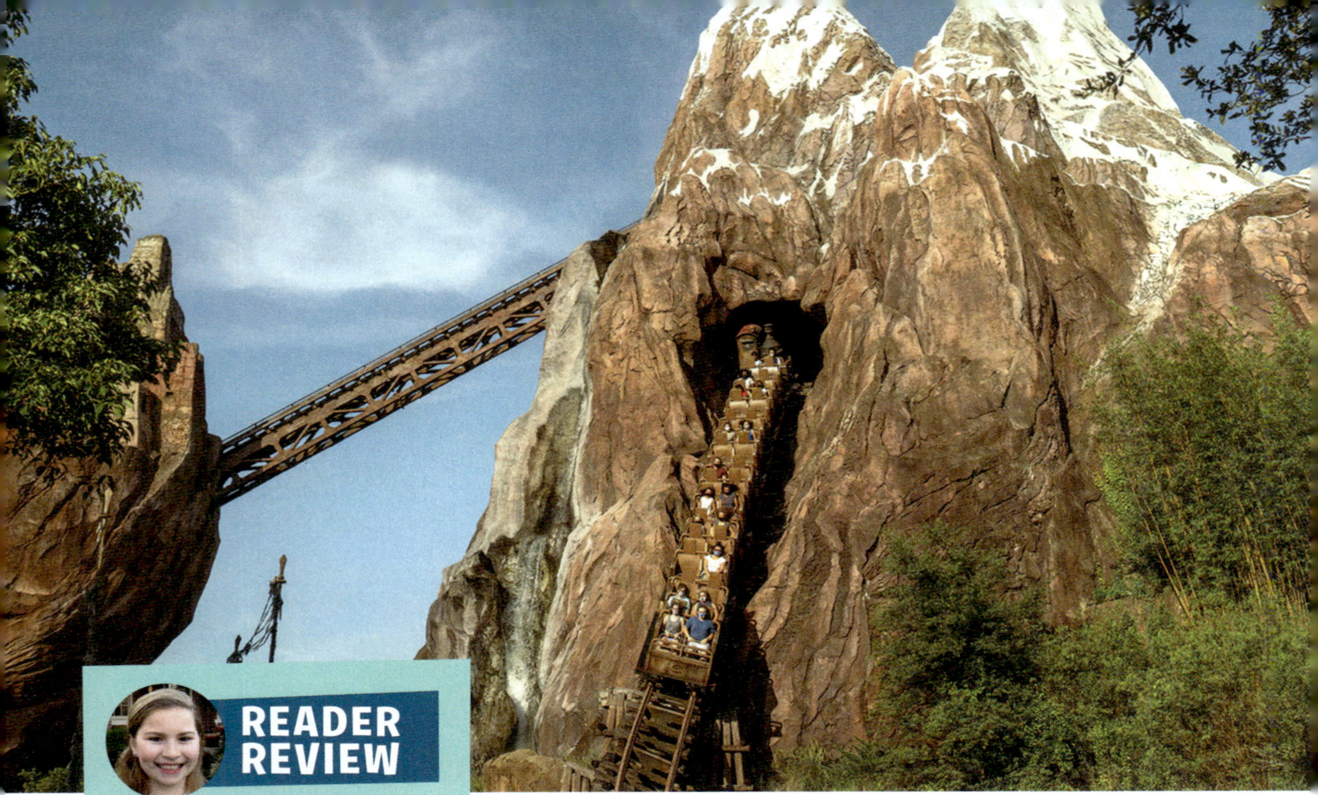

Expedition Everest

Mount Everest is the tallest mountain in the world. Can you guess the name of the tallest mountain in Walt Disney World? If you said Expedition Everest, you are right! Of course, it is much more than a mountain. It's a thrilling train ride through forests and waterfalls and over snow-capped mountain peaks. This ride is a lot rougher than Big Thunder Mountain Railroad. Here, you not only travel forward and backward through caverns and canyons, you also pass an angry yeti (that's an abominable snowman). His job is to protect the mountain from you!

This attraction is not for everyone. If you love wild, crazy, dark, and scary rides — and are at least 44 inches tall — give it a try. And be sure to say hello to the yeti for us!

#2 RIDE
Reader Pleaser

WILD DARK SCARY

YOU MUST BE AT LEAST 44 INCHES TALL TO RIDE EXPEDITION EVEREST.

Kali River Rapids

This is one of the wettest and wildest rides in Walt Disney World. (Don't bother trying to pick a dry seat on the raft, because there aren't any.) It begins as a peaceful trip through a rainforest. But things don't stay calm for very long. The raft bumps along down the river, spinning and turning every time it hits a wall.

Along the way you catch a glimpse of how logging (cutting down trees for lumber) can destroy the rainforest. Don't be scared if you see a fire — that's just part of the ride. You avoid the burning logs, but will you really go under that big waterfall? We won't tell. But you might want to bring a towel, just in case.

WILD

WET

YOU MUST BE AT LEAST 38 INCHES TALL TO RIDE KALI RIVER RAPIDS.

READER TIP

"Everything you carry on Kali River Rapids will get soaked. And so will you!"

— Drew (age 12), Jenison, MI

HOT TIP!

Want to keep your stuff dry while you ride Kali River Rapids? Leave it in a locker near the ride's entrance. Lockers are free for up to 2 hours.

READER REVIEW

I really like Kali River Rapids — especially on a hot day. You get soaked! And you never know who is going to get wet under a waterfall. If you want to stay dry, wear a poncho. It's a crazy river ride.

— Rian (age 8), Chantilly, VA

Feathered Friends in Flight

Live birds are the stars of this show in the Asia section of the park. They swoop and soar and do amazing tricks. The show is fun for all ages and presented several times a day. It lasts about 25 minutes. Don't leave right away — sometimes a handler will bring a bird out to meet guests.

The high-flying action happens in the Anandapur (say: *ah-NAHN-dah-purr*) Theater. Don't be surprised if a bird flies right over you! (Don't worry, all the birds in the show are very friendly.) The seating area is covered, but it does not have air-conditioning.

Details about this show may change this year. Ask a parent to check *disneyworld.com* for updates.

WHO AM I?

- **I love to bounce.**
- **I live in the Hundred Acre Wood.**
- **I'm the only one!**

Answer: Tigger

Pandora — The World of Avatar

Disney's Animal Kingdom has a special land called Pandora — The World of Avatar. It is a beautiful area that celebrates nature and all animal life. It has floating mountains, bridges, waterfalls, and plants. Many of the plants glow at night! The area has two attractions to enjoy: Na'vi River Journey and Avatar Flight of Passage.

Avatar Flight of Passage

Who said you need wings to fly? Just climb aboard a Mountain Banshee and soar over Pandora in this exciting thrill ride. It is sure to please most kids — especially the daredevils. In case you are wondering: A Mountain Banshee is a flying creature that looks like a dragon. It is also known as an Ikran (say: *EEK-rahn*).

Meet your avatar

Mountain Banshees don't like humans — that's why all guests need avatars (*AV-eh-tars*). Your avatar will ride the Ikran's back while you sit on something that's like a motorcycle seat. Everyone wears 3-D glasses, too.

Fly, Ikran, fly!

As the adventure begins, the powerful creature zooms through the air — and you're along for the ride. Hang on! Most kids agree that this is an amazing experience — so it is very popular. Get there early if you can. If heights or motion make you feel uncomfortable, you should skip this attraction.

WILD

LOUD

YOU MUST BE AT LEAST 44 INCHES TALL TO RIDE AVATAR FLIGHT OF PASSAGE.

READER REVIEW

Flight of Passage is the best ride in the world! It feels like you are actually riding on a living creature. My dream to temporarily run away from Earth and ride a Banshee has come true!

— Kathleen (age 12), Normal, IL

Na'vi River Journey

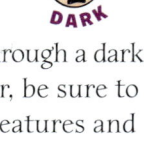

DARK

The Na'vi River Journey is a peaceful boat ride through a dark, glowing jungle. As you float on a mysterious river, be sure to notice all the details. Expect to see interesting creatures and glowing plants. You'll also see (and hear) an Audio-Animatronics character called the Shaman of Song. She is gigantic! This journey is a nice way to take a cool break on a hot day.

The Oasis

The Oasis is a small, green area at the front of Animal Kingdom. It is a lot like an oasis in a desert. It has pretty plants and flowing water. It's also home to some of the park's coolest critters. There's wildlife to discover on both sides of the Oasis. You can check out one side as you enter and the other side as you leave the park.

The Oasis Exhibits

The Oasis is home to many animals. Some are easier to spot than others. They hang out in areas called exhibits. That means they are there for you to admire. You may spy creatures that fly and some that swim — and some that do both! You should keep an eye out for a giant anteater, boar, barking deer, and wallabies. Some of the animals are shy and like to hide. Others play in the open. Be sure to have a camera ready.

Entertainment

Animal Kingdom has some very talented performers. Some walk on two legs, while others walk on four — or eight. There are lots of shows every day. There are drummers, musicians, live animals, and many other things to entertain you. Read about some of them below.

PHOTO BY JILL SAFRO

Winged Encounters — The Kingdom Takes Flight

Look up and you might see colorful parrots flying over your head! They spread their wings above Discovery Island several times a day. Bird care experts are there, too. They like to answer questions and share interesting facts.

Viva Gaia Street Band

Put your dancing shoes on and head to Discovery Island for an exciting musical show. In it, band members invite guests to join their Caribbean street party! The show lasts about 30 minutes. It usually happens early in the day.

Harambe Village Entertainment

Musicians dance and play drums in the park's Harambe Village. A team of acrobats may perform there, too. The shows are fun for everyone.

Kora Tinga Tinga

A kora is a hand-made African harp with 21 strings. You can hear one played in Disney's Animal Kingdom. The musician is very talented. He comes from a family that has performed for kings!

Di-Vine

You may think your eyes are playing tricks on you when you see this giant plant wandering through the park. The plant is actually a human performer walking on stilts. Very cool!

Tree of Life Awakenings

When the park is open after dark, the Tree of Life wakes up covered in lights and pictures of animals. The colorful show takes place every ten minutes. It covers the Tree of Life on all sides — so it's easy to see. Watching this show is a nice way to end the day.

Where to Find Characters
at Disney's Animal Kingdom

It's fun to search for characters at Disney's Animal Kingdom. **Adventurers Outpost** on Discovery Island is a good place to find Mickey Mouse and Minnie Mouse. Moana greets fellow voyagers on **Discovery Island**. You may spot Kevin walking around, too!

Donald Duck, Daisy Duck, Pluto, Russell, Dug, Chip, Dale, Pocahontas, and friends from *The Lion King* may also greet guests around the park. (Characters from *The Lion King* perform in a show called Festival of The Lion King, too.)

Disney characters love to pose for photos, so have your camera ready. And ask them to sign the autograph pages at the back of this book!

Details may change at any time. For updates, ask a parent to visit *disneyworld.com*.

TIPS

Animal Kingdom can get very warm, especially in summer months. Head for Festival of the Lion King, Finding Nemo, Kali River Rapids, or Rafiki's Planet Watch to cool off. And don't forget to drink lots of water.

Go to Avatar Flight of Passage, Na'vi River Journey, and Expedition Everest early — before they get too crowded.

On the Kilimanjaro Safaris ride, look at the chart over your head. The pictures will show which animals you're about to see.

Can't find your parents? Ask a Disney cast member for help. (A cast member is a park worker wearing a name tag).

It doesn't really matter what time you get to the Kilimanjaro Safaris ride — the animals are there all day long.

A baby tiger was born at Animal Kingdom in 2024! His name is Bakso, and he is adorable. You can see him and his mother, Sohni, on Maharajah Jungle Trek. Try to get there early; Bakso has lots of fans!

It's fun to see how many animals you can find carved into The Tree of Life. Some folks use binoculars.

Look for Mickey and Minnie at the Adventurers Outpost on Discovery Island. And don't forget your camera!

There's a big painting at the entrance of Conservation Station at Rafiki's Planet Watch. It's filled with animal images and Hidden Mickeys. How many can you find?

Stash your stuff in a locker before you ride Kali River Rapids — unless you don't mind if your things get wet.

Attraction Ratings

COOL
(Check it out!)

- The Oasis (the area inside the park entrance)
- Affection Section (at Rafiki's Planet Watch)
- Adventurers Outpost
- The Boneyard playground
- Zootopia: Better Zoogether

VERY COOL
(Don't miss!)

- Na'vi River Journey
- Feathered Friends in Flight
- Maharajah Jungle Trek
- Gorilla Falls Exploration Trail
- Finding Nemo: The Big Blue . . . and Beyond!
- Drawn to Magic (at Rafiki's Planet Watch)

COOLEST
(See at least twice!)

- Expedition Everest
- Avatar Flight of Passage
- Kilimanjaro Safaris
- Kali River Rapids
- Festival of the Lion King
- Dinosaur

YOUR FAVORITE ANIMAL KINGDOM ATTRACTIONS

_____   _____
_____   _____
_____   _____

Everything Else in the World

No matter what you are interested in — water fun, sports, or animals — Walt Disney World has enough to make every minute of your vacation a blast. After you visit the theme parks, there's still so much to do. There are water parks, canoes to rent, horses to ride, fish to catch, and lots of neat shopping spots.

If you are into sports, you may want to check out the ESPN Wide World of Sports Complex, rent a bicycle, or try some mini golf. Are you a fan of Disney movies? You can watch them outdoors, under the stars at a Disney hotel.

In this chapter, you can read up on all the extra activities and find out about hotels and restaurants at Walt Disney World. Then you can help your family decide where to stay, where to eat, and what to do when you are not visiting the theme parks.

Waters of the World

It's easy to get wet, stay cool, and have fun at Walt Disney World. That's because it's a water wonderland. Choose a water park or swim in your hotel pool. (If you are younger than age 14 and you want to visit a water park, you must go with a guest who is older than 14.)

Typhoon Lagoon

A typhoon is a powerful, wet, and windy storm. It dumps huge amounts of rain and sends objects flying through the air. This water park looks like a typhoon blew through it. There's even a boat stuck on a mountaintop! Of course, a storm didn't really put the boat there — Disney Imagineers did. They also put in pools, water slides, and a raft ride.

Catch the wave

The big pool here is like a small ocean. It has 6-foot waves! There are speed slides to try, too. In the mood for a big thrill? If you are at least 48 inches tall, try Crush 'n' Gusher. It's like a water roller coaster. For a calmer experience, you can hop into a tube and float along a lazy river. There is also a special area just for younger kids — Ketchakiddee Creek. It has small slides and other games. You must be 48 inches or shorter to play in Ketchakiddee Creek (and have a grown-up with you).

Miss Adventure Falls

Miss Adventure Falls is a wild water ride for the whole family — up to four people can travel in each raft. It is the longest ride ever built at a Disney World water park. Hold on tight! During the 2-minute trip, you will spy lots of sparkly things. Keep your eyes out for a treasure-hunting parrot.

HOT TIP!

The water is heated at Walt Disney World pools and water parks — so you can swim all year long. Be sure to take warm cover-ups for chilly days — Disney doesn't heat the air!

Blizzard Beach

Would you wear a swimsuit to a snow-covered mountain? Probably not. But you should wear one to Blizzard Beach. It looks like a place to ski, but it's really a splashy water park. So don't worry if you can't ski. Nobody skis down the mountains here. They slide!

Reach the peak

Like a real ski resort, the action centers around a mountain. In this case, it is Mount Gushmore. To get to the top, you can take a chairlift. The ride gives you a great view of the park. The scariest slide on the mountain is Summit Plummet. It begins 120 feet in the air, on a platform that looks like a ski jump. It drops you down a steep slide at about 60 miles per hour. That's faster than some cars go on the highway! You can ride Summit Plummet if you are at least 48 inches tall.

Slip-sliding away

There are plenty of ways to slide down the mountain. Tube slides, body slides, and inner-tube rides can keep you busy all day long. It's fun to splash in the wave pool, too. For preteens, there's Ski Patrol Training Camp, with its "iceberg" obstacle course and ropes for swinging into the water. Tike's Peak is a special place for younger kids. It has slides and a snow-castle fountain play area — all with a *Frozen* theme. Say hi to the Snowgies for us!

READER TIP

"Go to a water park early in the day — when it's hot and crowded at the theme parks. Then you can return to the theme park when it cools down in the evening."

— David (age 14), Calabasas, CA

HOT TIP!

Bring water shoes to Walt Disney World water parks. That way, you won't burn your feet when you walk around. The ground can get super hot in the summer months!

Fort Wilderness

Fort Wilderness is tucked away in a woodsy area of Walt Disney World. (It isn't really a fort. It's a campground.) You can stay the night or come for a day. There are tennis and volleyball courts, and playgrounds to explore. You could spend days here and not run out of things to do. If you have time, stop at the pony farm or rent a bike with a parent.

Pony Farm

There is a small farm at Fort Wilderness. It's a short walk from Pioneer Hall. There is no charge to visit the farm, but it costs about $10 for a pony ride. Be sure to bring a grown-up with you. If you don't want to ride a pony, you can still stop by and say hello. Most visitors think a trip to the farm is a fun way to spend some time away from the parks.

YOU MUST BE LESS THAN 48 INCHES TALL TO RIDE A PONY AT WALT DISNEY WORLD.

More Fort Wilderness Fun

Fort Wilderness offers lots of other things to do. You can rent a canoe for a trip along a canal. Or you can rent a bicycle and explore the trails. At the Tri-Circle-D Ranch, you can visit the horses that pull the trolleys in the Magic Kingdom. (The horses live in a big barn near Pioneer Hall.)

Kids age 9 and older can take a trail ride on horseback. With a parent, kids can also enjoy a wagon ride, do some fishing, or roast marshmallows at a campfire.

Sports

Kids who like sports can find plenty of ways to keep active at Walt Disney World. You can rent boats and bikes at a resort, or play mini golf on a themed course. To see athletes at work, visit ESPN Wide World of Sports Complex. Read on to find out how.

ESPN Wide World of Sports Complex

Sports nuts might enjoy a visit to this place. It has space for every sport you can think of — including field hockey, soccer, gymnastics, cheer, and more. You can spend a whole day watching some amateur sporting events.

Tickets to the Wide World of Sports complex cost about $15 for kids ages 3 to 9 and about $20 for anyone 10 or older. If you want to attend a special event, you will have to buy tickets ahead of time. A parent should call 407-939-4263 for tickets.

Archery

Guests can learn archery at Disney's Fort Wilderness resort — as long as they are at least 7 years old. Each class lasts about 75 minutes. Archery guides will teach you how to use a bow and aim your arrow at a target. It's not as easy as Merida makes it look in the movie *Brave*! But most kids get the hang of it with a little practice.

The class costs $49 per person (plus tax). Ask a grown-up to visit *disneyworld.com* to learn more about the Fort Wilderness Archery Experience.

Miniature Golf

Even if you have never held a golf club before, you may enjoy mini golf. It's fun to play and full of surprises.

Fantasia Gardens

If you've seen the classic movie *Fantasia*, you will know how this miniature golf course got its name. Where else would you find hippos on tiptoe, dancing mushrooms, or xylophone stairs?

The holes are grouped by musical themes. At the Dance of the Hours hole, watch the hippopotamus standing on an alligator. If you hit a golf ball through the gator's mouth, the hippo dances!

The cost is about $12 to play one round for kids ages 3 to 9 and about $19 for anyone 10 or older.

Disney's Winter Summerland

Sometimes Santa Claus needs a vacation. Just like you, he has picked Walt Disney World as the perfect place to have fun!

As the story goes, Santa and his helpers built these mini-golf courses as a place to relax and enjoy the sun. That's why one looks like a beach, with sand castles and surfboards on it. But then the elves got homesick, so they built a second course that reminded them of the North Pole. Everything looks like it is covered in snow. There are even igloos, jolly snow people, and holes for ice fishing.

For a bit of a challenge, try the summer course. It's a little harder than the winter course. Santa is snoozing at one of the trickiest holes. You have to hit the ball across his belly without waking him up. The winter holes offer surprises, too.

To play on one course, it costs about $12 for kids ages 3 to 9 and about $19 for folks age 10 or older.

Waiting Games

Walt Disney World is packed with fun shows and attractions — and they are popular with kids of all ages. That means there's usually a wait to get in. Of course, no one loves to wait in line. But there is a way to make the time fly by. Play the games on this page!

PLAY DISNEY PARKS APP

Play Disney Parks is a free app for a mobile phone. It has games that you can play while waiting in line for Disney shows and attractions. Be sure to get a parent's permission before you download the app. You can read more about it on page 88 of this book.

THE ALPHABET GAME

You may want to practice your ABCs before you start this game. In it, you'll go through the alphabet, with players taking turns naming Disney characters. A is for Aladdin. B is for Baloo. C is for Cinderella. And so on. If you make it all the way to Zazu or Zurg, it's time to start over!

HINT: If you get stuck, it helps to think of the characters in your favorite Disney films. Some kids like to include Walt Disney World shows and attractions, too.

HIDDEN MICKEY HUNT

This one is easy. Just look around and search for images of Mickey Mouse. Look on signs, walls, lamps, ceilings. Mickey can be anywhere! Some kids like to count mouse ear hats, Mickey shirts, toys, and balloons, too. How many Mickeys can you discover?

WHO AM I?

Think of a Disney character (but don't say the name out loud). Tell your family members to ask questions to help them guess who you are. They can ask "yes" or "no" questions such as "Are you an animal?" or "Can you fly?" You should answer with YES or NO. When someone guesses your character, they win! The winner gets to start the next round. Now it's your turn to ask questions.

I SPY

You may have played the I Spy game before — but have you ever played it in a Disney theme park? Now's your chance. First choose an object that your family can see. Then give a clue about its color or the letter it begins with. Say "I spy with my little eye something that is red." Everyone gets to shout out guesses. When someone gets it right, they win. The winner gets to pick the next clue.

WRITE A DISNEY STORY

Write a Disney story with your family. The first line could be: *Minnie is throwing a surprise party for Mickey at EPCOT.* What could follow that? Each person adds a line to the story. It can be as long or short as you want. When it is finished, say "and they lived happily ever after" or "the end!"

Disney Springs

Disney Springs is a great place to visit on a non-park day. It has shops, games, movies, restaurants, and much more. There are areas to explore and lots to discover — like life-like dinosaurs and cars that are also boats. Some spots offer live entertainment. There are four neighborhoods at Disney Springs: Town Center, Marketplace, The West Side, and The Landing. Town Center is a big shopping mall. Read on to learn about the other areas.

The West Side

This zone has places to shop, eat, bowl, watch a movie, and hear live music. It also has a huge balloon that takes guests for rides high in the sky. (You will need a ticket and a grown-up to go with you.) It's fun to watch even if you don't ride.

Marketplace

Searching for a souvenir? Head straight to the Marketplace. There are lots of shops there. One place that kids enjoy is World of Disney.

It's a shop with Disney-themed goodies. Nearby, you can dig for fossils in a dino-themed restaurant or check out giant statues made out of LEGOs. They are very cool.

The Landing

This neighborhood has waterside shops and snack spots. It's also where the Amphicars are. They are cars that float! (Each costs about $125 and can fit up to 4 guests.) It's fun to watch the cars drive into the water!

Electrical Water Pageant

Have you ever seen a parade on a lake? Now is your chance. The Electrical Water Pageant is Disney's floating parade. The pageant made its magical debut in October 1971. It was part of the grand opening of the Polynesian Village Resort. Walt Disney World was 3 weeks old at the time.

Above the sea

The water parade takes place on the Seven Seas Lagoon (the lake next to the Magic Kingdom) and on Bay Lake (behind the Contemporary resort hotel). The nightly show has thousands of sparkling lights on connected floats. The floats have screens that show King Triton and other sea creatures — turtles, seahorses, an octopus, and a sea serpent. It's all set to Disney music. The pageant may be canceled when the weather is windy or stormy.

The end of the parade is a tribute to America. That's when the lights become flags and stars. The finale has a patriotic music medley, too. If you know the words to "You're a Grand Old Flag" and "Yankee Doodle Dandy," feel free to sing along.

Catch it if you can!

You can see the Electrical Water Pageant from many places around Bay Lake and the Seven Seas Lagoon. (The lakes near the Magic Kingdom park.) Each water parade lasts about 15 minutes. The start times change during the year. The first show usually happens soon after the Magic Kingdom fireworks end. Here is a list of places to watch the Electrical Water Pageant:

- Polynesian Village Resort
- Grand Floridian Resort
- Wilderness Lodge
- Disney's Fort Wilderness Resort and Campground
- Contemporary Resort
- On nights when the Magic Kingdom is open late, the show takes place right outside the park entrance.

Walt Disney World Resort Hotels

There are more than 25 hotels at Walt Disney World. There are so many hotel rooms that you could stay in a different one every night for 68 years! Just like the rides at the parks, each of the resorts has its own special theme. And it's fun to stay at all of the hotels. But it can be nice just to visit, too. So if you have time, you might want to stop by some of them. You can have a snack or just enjoy the fun atmosphere.

Resorts near the Magic Kingdom

Contemporary

This was the first-ever Walt Disney World hotel. It looked very modern when it was built in 1971. And it still looks cool more than fifty years later! When the hotel opened, it had a talking elevator and a monorail station right in the middle of it. It still has the monorail, plus a fun pool and Chef Mickey's — a place to have a meal and meet Mickey Mouse and his pals.

CONTEMPORARY TIP
In the center of the resort is a 3-sided mural that's 90 feet tall. There are colorful pictures of children and animals all over it. One of the goats has five legs. See how long it takes you to find it.

Fort Wilderness

Stay in a camper, tent, or cabin at this pretty campground. This resort has many activities. You can go for a wagon ride, visit a pony farm, or take a trip through the woods on a horse. At night, Chip and Dale sometimes roast marshmallows by a campfire. This is also home to a popular dinner show called the Hoop-Dee-Doo Musical Revue.

FORT WILDERNESS TIP
The horses that pull trolleys in the Magic Kingdom live in a stable at Fort Wilderness. You can visit for free. You can also peek at the Dragon Calliope. It's a big musical instrument that's pulled by horses. Walt Disney bought it in the 1950s and used it in a Disneyland parade.

Wilderness Lodge

With its big log columns and totem poles, this hotel looks like a national park from the American Northwest. The fireplaces and rocking chairs in the main building make you feel right at home. There is an indoor stream and a bridge. Outside, there is an erupting geyser and a pool. There are so many Hidden Mickeys here that there's a contest to see how many you can find.

WILDERNESS LODGE TIP
The fireplace in the main lobby is 82 feet tall! It was built to look like part of the Grand Canyon. That's why it's called the Grand Canyon fireplace. Can you spot the Hidden Mickey at the top?

Polynesian Village

The plants and trees at this hotel make it look like a tropical island. The greenery and cheery colors in the main building make the setting seem real even when you're indoors. There's a pool that looks like it is made from lava from a volcano, and a beach to relax on. The WDW monorail makes a stop here, too.

POLYNESIAN VILLAGE TIP
Grab a snack (and your family) and have a picnic on or near the beach. Then enjoy the fireworks over the Magic Kingdom — the show's music plays all around you! It's a great way to end a Disney day.

Grand Floridian

This hotel looks like a huge mansion from the early 1900s. At first, it seems to be for adults, but it's also fun for kids. There may be activities like storytelling and crafts. Or you can sit in a comfy chair and listen to a piano played in the lobby. There are two pools: one is surrounded by roses and the other has a waterfall. There is an *Alice in Wonderland* splash zone, too. The monorail stops here.

GRAND FLORIDIAN TIP
In November and December, the Grand Floridian is home to a giant gingerbread house. It is made with real gingerbread and so big that a few grown-up people can fit inside!

PHOTO BY JILL SAFRO

THE MONORAIL

The monorail connects the Magic Kingdom park with the Contemporary, Polynesian Village, and Grand Floridian resorts. It's also a neat way to travel from the Magic Kingdom park to EPCOT. Just switch monorail trains when you get to the Transportation and Ticket Center. (The Transportation and Ticket Center is also called the T.T.C.)

Resorts near EPCOT and Disney's Hollywood Studios

BoardWalk

This hotel is designed to look the way Atlantic City, New Jersey, once did. Just like one on an old-fashioned boardwalk, there are games and snack stands here for all to enjoy. You can rent a special bicycle built for four. And you can splash in a pool zone that looks like an amusement park.

BOARDWALK TIP
Disney's BoardWalk is a very entertaining resort. Look for performers out on the boardwalk in the evening hours. And be sure to visit the resort's backyard. That's where "Movies Under the Stars" are shown at night.

Port Orleans — French Quarter

Details at this hotel make it look as if it is in New Orleans, Louisiana. There's a long river and a cool pool. The pool has a water slide that looks like a sea serpent's tongue.

PORT ORLEANS — FRENCH QUARTER TIP
After taking a dip in the French Quarter pool, you may want to visit the pool at Port Orleans Riverside. You can walk or hop on a Walt Disney World bus. Be sure to take your parents with you!

Port Orleans — Riverside

This hotel's buildings look like historic homes from southern U.S. states. There is a big water-wheel inside the food court. It's 30 feet tall! The pool is on Ol' Man Island, an area that was inspired by the story of Tom Sawyer. You can rent a fishing pole there, too.

PORT ORLEANS — RIVERSIDE TIP

If you like to fish, head down to the Fishin' Hole at Ol' Man Island. The recreation area has fishing poles to rent and bait to buy.

Caribbean Beach

Happy and colorful, this hotel looks like resorts on some Caribbean islands. You can have fun in the sun all day at its pools and playgrounds. There is a cool splash area and pool slide. And the pool has a pirate theme!

CARIBBEAN BEACH TIP

The hotel has a bike path that circles a lake. It's more than a mile long! Bikes can be rented at the marina. (Helmets may be borrowed for free.)

Riviera

Walt Disney loved traveling through Europe. The Riviera hotel is based on what he saw during his visits. You can find bubbling fountains, quiet gardens, and beautiful artwork to enjoy.

RIVIERA TIP

There's lots of outdoor fun to be had here. Kids love the splash zone by the pool. You can play a bowling type game called bocce (pronounced *bah-CHEE*), lawn chess, and other games, too.

Old Key West

The town houses that make up this resort have all the comforts of home. The palm trees and sunny design make it a warm and welcoming place. And the pool has an awesome slide.

OLD KEY WEST TIP

Kids of all ages enjoy the crafts and games at Community Hall. The wet and wild games at the main swimming pool are lots of fun, too.

READER TIP

"The TVs in Disney hotel rooms have a special channel that is all about Walt Disney World. Don't miss it!"

— Nicholas (age 9), Mount Pleasant, SC

Pop Century Resort

The twentieth century might be over, but it is hard to forget when you visit this hotel. Giant pieces of art (like old cell phones and jukeboxes) decorate the buildings. The hotel pays tribute to each decade from the 1950s to the 1990s.

POP CENTURY TIP

On hot days, you can cool off by splashing under the flower-shaped water jets.

Saratoga Springs Resort

This hotel is designed to look like a town in upstate New York in the late 1800s. There are lots of pretty gardens to look at. But the best views come from a special lakeside spot. From there you can see the lights of Disney Springs. The pools here are a blast!

SARATOGA SPRINGS TIP

The hotel has 2 cool pool areas! Each spot has at least one big water slide. The High Rock pool also has a splash zone and a mini water slide.

Yacht and Beach Club

These hotels are meant to look like the homes near the beaches of Massachusetts. Even the pool makes it feel as if you're at the beach — the bottom is covered with sand.

YACHT AND BEACH CLUB TIP

Pack comfy walking shoes. One of the best parts about staying here is that you can walk to EPCOT, Disney's Hollywood Studios, and the BoardWalk resort.

Swan and Dolphin

You can't miss the dolphin and swan statues that sit on top of these hotels — they are huge. There's a lot to do at the Swan and Dolphin. The pool area is a ton of fun. And you can walk or take a FriendShip boat to EPCOT, Disney's Hollywood Studios, and the BoardWalk resort from the hotels.

SWAN AND DOLPHIN TIP

There are 250 swan and dolphin statues at this resort. Some are big, but some are very small. See how many you can spot.

PHOTO BY JILL SAFRO

Art of Animation

This resort celebrates animation. And if you are a fan of *Finding Nemo*, *The Little Mermaid*, *The Lion King*, or *Cars*, you are going to love it here. Be sure to look up — there are tons of giant character statues. Super cool!

ART OF ANIMATION TIP

There is no water slide, but kids still love the pools at this resort. Don't miss the splash zone in the *Finding Nemo* courtyard. It's a great place to have fun with a younger brother or sister.

Resorts near Disney's Animal Kingdom

Coronado Springs

This hotel celebrates the daring spirit of Spanish explorers, artists, and writers. The buildings are the color of clay. The pool looks like an ancient pyramid, with a slide that passes under a spitting jaguar. Beside it is a playground with ancient treasures waiting to be discovered.

CORONADO SPRINGS TIP

The resort has a play area called The Explorers Zone. It is designed to look like Aztec ruins. Kids ages 2 to 12 may enjoy its slides, jungle gym, and dig site.

All-Star Resorts

There are three All-Star resorts, and each one of them has a theme — sports, music, or movies. It's easy to tell which All-Star hotel you are visiting because they have giant icons that are bigger than the buildings. At All-Star Music, look for giant cowboy boots. A huge football helmet means you are at All-Star Sports. And when you see a 38-foot-tall Buzz Lightyear, there's no doubt you are at All-Star Movies.

ALL-STAR TIP

There are a whole lot of Hidden Mickeys to hunt for at these hotels! Start your search at the main statue in each resort.

Animal Kingdom Lodge

Creatures like giraffes, zebras, gazelles, and beautiful birds live near this hotel — and they are all real. The trees and animals make it seem as if the resort is set in an African savanna. A giant mud fireplace and thatched roofs add to the feeling that you really are in Africa.

ANIMAL KINGDOM LODGE TIP

Almost all of the rooms at Animal Kingdom Lodge have good views of the animals. But if you want an even closer look, remember to bring some binoculars from home.

READER TIP

"If you stay at a Disney hotel, be sure to ask for a wake-up call. It is usually Mickey Mouse or Stitch."

— Raquel (age 7), Miami, FL

MOVIES UNDER THE STARS

There are lots of fun things for kids to enjoy at Walt Disney World resorts. One of them is called Movies Under the Stars. On most nights, a Disney film is shown outdoors. Sometimes there is a campfire and marshmallow roast before the show. You can get a movie schedule at your hotel's front desk. (The movie may be moved indoors or canceled if the weather is bad.)

HOT TIP!

Movies Under the Stars can be extra special at Disney's Fort Wilderness resort. Chip and Dale may stop by to say hello before the movie begins!

Restaurants

Eating at Walt Disney World can be as much fun as riding Space Mountain (well, almost as much fun!). Here are our ideas for the best spots in each theme park to head to for your favorite foods.

 **HOT TIP!**

There are lots of healthier and yummy food choices for kids at Walt Disney World. Just look for a check symbol on the menu. And remember to drink a lot of water while out in the hot Florida sun.

MAGIC KINGDOM
Best Places for Favorite Foods

Breadsticks (with tomato sauce) . . . . Pinocchio Village Haus

Candied apples . . . . Main Street Confectionery

Cookies . . . . Main Street Confectionery

Fruit . . . . Liberty Square Market

Hamburgers . . . . Cosmic Ray's Starlight Cafe

Hot dogs . . . . Casey's Corner

Ice cream . . . . Plaza Ice Cream Parlor

LeFou's Brew (apple slush drink) . . . . Gaston's Tavern

Macaroni and cheese . . . . The Friar's Nook

Pizza . . . . Pinocchio Village Haus

Pretzels . . . . Fantasyland Pretzel Stand (in Storybook Circus)

Shakes & Smoothies . . . . Auntie Gravity's Galactic Goodies

Tacos . . . . Pecos Bill Tall Tale Inn

Turkey legs . . . . Frontierland Turkey Leg Cart

EPCOT
Best Places for Favorite Foods

Candy and cookies . . . . **Karamell-Küche (in Germany)**

Cheeseburgers . . . . **Connections Eatery (in World Celebration)**

Egg rolls . . . . **Lotus Blossom Cafe (in China)**

Fruit . . . . **Sunshine Seasons (in The Land)**

Hot dogs . . . . **Fife and Drum Tavern (in The American Adventure)**

Ice cream . . . . **L'Artisan des Glaces (in France)**

Jumbo pretzels . . . . **The Pretzel Wagon (in Germany)**

Macaroni and cheese . . . . **Sunshine Seasons (in The Land)**

Pasta with tomato sauce . . . . **Via Napoli (in Italy)**

Pastries . . . . **Les Halles Boulangerie Patisserie (in France)**

Peanut butter and jelly sandwiches . . . . . . **Sunshine Seasons (in The Land)**

Pizza . . . . **Via Napoli (in Italy)**

Tacos . . . . **La Cantina de San Angel (in Mexico)**

Turkey legs . . . . **Fife and Drum Tavern (in The American Adventure)**

DISNEY'S HOLLYWOOD STUDIOS
Best Places for Favorite Foods

Chicken noodle soup . . . . Sci-Fi Dine-In Theater

Chicken strips . . . . Backlot Express

Churros . . . . Anaheim Produce (in Sunset Ranch Market)

Fruit . . . . Anaheim Produce (in Sunset Ranch Market)

Grilled cheese . . . . Woody's Lunch Box (in Toy Story Land)

Ice cream . . . . Hollywood Scoops (in Sunset Ranch Market)

Macaroni and cheese . . . . Backlot Express

Milk shakes . . . . Dockside Diner

Peanut butter and jelly sandwiches . . . . Backlot Express

Pickle in a pouch . . . . Anaheim Produce (in Sunset Ranch Market)

Pizza . . . . Catalina Eddie's (in Sunset Ranch Market)

Root beer floats . . . . Epic Eats (Echo Lake area)

Tacos . . . . ABC Commissary

Turkey sandwiches . . . . Woody's Lunch Box (in Toy Story Land)

DISNEY'S ANIMAL KINGDOM
Best Places for Favorite Foods

Barbecued ribs and chicken . . . . **Flame Tree Barbecue**

Breadsticks (with tomato sauce) . . . . **Pizzafari**

Cheeseburgers . . . . **Restaurantosaurus**

Cheese quesadilla . . . . **Satu'li Canteen**

Chicken nuggets and fries . . . . **Restaurantosaurus**

Corn-on-the-cob . . . . **Harambe Fruit Market**

Dole Whip (frozen pineapple treat) . . . . **Tamu Tamu Refreshments**

Egg rolls . . . . **Yak and Yeti Local Food Cafes**

Fruit . . . . **Harambe Fruit Market**

Grilled cheese . . . . **Rainforest Cafe**

Hot dogs . . . . **Flame Tree Barbecue**

Ice cream . . . . **Anandapur Ice Cream Truck**

Mac and cheese . . . . **Restaurantosaurus**

Mickey-shaped pretzels . . . . **Dino-Bite Snacks**

Pizza . . . . **Pizzafari**

Eating with Disney Characters

Kids of all ages enjoy eating with the characters. It's one of the best ways to meet your favorite Disney stars. Bring a camera because the characters are also happy to pose for photos. They love to be up close, or in the background of your selfies!

Each of the theme parks has at least one restaurant that invites the characters over. Many of the resorts have character meals, too. They are very popular, so no matter which restaurant your family chooses, it's a good idea to make reservations far ahead of time. (Ask a parent to visit *disneyworld.com/dining*.)

Character meals aren't fun just because you get to meet the characters. They are also special because the food is yummy! Picky eaters may enjoy buffet-style meals — with so much to choose from, there's something for everyone. Details may change at any time.

Dinner Shows

Hoop-Dee-Doo Musical Revue

Entertainers sing, dance, and tell jokes while you chow down on chicken, ribs, and veggies. If you go, be prepared to clap your hands, stomp your feet, and sing along. The jokes are silly, but everyone always has a good time. The food is tasty, too. That's probably why the Hoop-Dee-Doo is a very popular dinner show at Walt Disney World.

Raglan Road

Every day is like Saint Patrick's Day at Raglan Road! The Irish restaurant has a kids menu and live entertainment. You can watch dancers and listen to an Irish band while you munch on your meal. You will find it at the Landing in Disney Springs. And in case you were wondering, the Irish word for dance is *damhsa* (say DOW-suh).

For reservations, a parent can visit *disneyworld.com/dining*, or call 407-938-0300.

MAGICAL MEMORIES

The fun doesn't have to end when your vacation does.
Use these pages to preserve your Disney memories.

These are the people I vacationed with:

I arrived at Walt Disney World on:

_____
Month / Day / Year

I stayed for _____ days.

On my first day at Walt Disney World, I went to:

The name of our hotel was:

My usual bedtime is _____ o'clock.

During my trip, the latest I went to bed was _____ o'clock!

The earliest I woke up was _____ o'clock.

I traveled to Walt Disney World by:

☐ car ☐ train

☐ bus ☐ ship

☐ plane ☐ flying carpet

If I were a Disney Imagineer, this is the ride I would make:

This attraction was not what I expected:

It surprised me because:

Draw your favorite Disney character here:

The weather at Walt Disney World was:

☐ sunny ☐ rainy

☐ cloudy ☐ cold

☐ windy

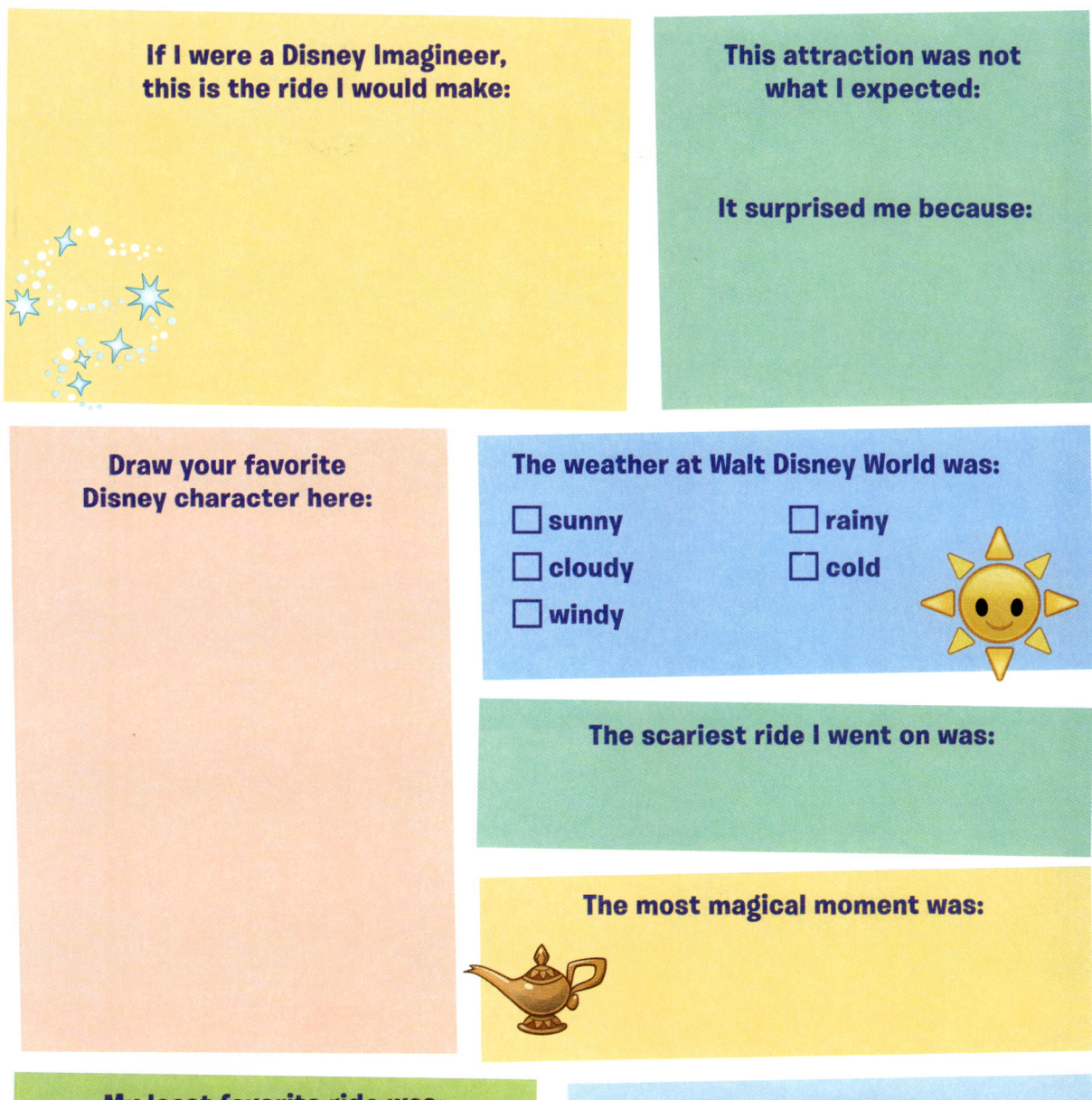

The scariest ride I went on was:

The most magical moment was:

My least favorite ride was:

I didn't like it because:

My favorite ride was:

I went on it _____ times.

Building a theme park was Walt Disney's dream. This is one of my dreams:

Vacations aren't just fun — they are educational, too. One thing I learned at Walt Disney World is:

The funniest thing that happened at Walt Disney World was:

Tape a Disney World vacation photo here:

The best Disney theme park was:

☐ **Magic Kingdom**

☐ **EPCOT**

☐ **Disney's Hollywood Studios**

☐ **Disney's Animal Kingdom**

My favorite Disney restaurant was:

I ate:

My favorite Walt Disney World snack is:

I found _____ Hidden Mickeys.

I met _____ characters during my vacation. The first character I met was:

My favorite character is:

It's fun to remember a vacation with souvenirs. One thing I brought home is:

Someday, I'll go back to Walt Disney World. The first thing I'll do when I get there is:

Autographs

Disney characters love to sign autographs. So take a pen and ask them to sign these pages for you. And have a family member take your picture with each character you see. That will help you remember the magical moments. You can print the photos and tape them to the pages of this book.

MICKEY MOUSE and MINNIE MOUSE

DONALD DUCK and DAISY DUCK

ANNA and ELSA

GOOFY and PLUTO

WOODY and BUZZ

AUTOGRAPHS

AUTOGRAPHS

AUTOGRAPHS

AUTOGRAPHS

AUTOGRAPHS

AUTOGRAPHS